WHEN GOD SAYS
WAR IS RIGHT

WHEN GOD SAYS WAR IS RIGHT

The Christian's Perspective
on When and How to Fight

DARRELL COLE

WATERBROOK
PRESS

WHEN GOD SAYS WAR IS RIGHT
PUBLISHED BY WATERBROOK PRESS
2375 Telstar Drive, Suite 160
Colorado Springs, Colorado 80920
A division of Random House, Inc.

ISBN 1-57856-657-6

Library of Congress Cataloging-in-Publication Data
Cole, Darrell.
    When God says war is right : the Christian's perspective on when and how to fight / by Darrell Cole.—1st ed.
       p. cm.
Includes bibliographical references (p. 159).
    ISBN 1-57856-657-6
      1. War—Religious aspects—Christianity. 2. Terrorism—Religious aspects—Christianity. I. Title.

BT736.2.C578 2002
241'.6242—dc21

                2002006400

Printed in the United States of America
2002—First Edition

10 9 8 7 6 5 4 3 2 1

In loving memory of my father—
a soldier in the Second World War, and a Christian

Contents

War is a dreadful thing, and I can respect an honest pacifist, though I think he is entirely mistaken. What I cannot understand is this sort of semi-pacifism you get nowadays which gives people the idea that though you have to fight, you ought to do it with a long face and as if you were ashamed of it.

—C. S. LEWIS, *MERE CHRISTIANITY*

It is characteristic nowadays to talk with horror of killing rather than of murder, and hence, since in war you have committed yourself to killing—for example "accepted evil"—not to mind whom you kill. This seems largely to be the work of the devil.

—G. E. M. ANSCOMBE, "MR. TRUMAN'S DEGREE"

A New and Old Question

Taking On the Moral Problems of War

Jesus Christ told His disciples to love their enemies and to turn the other cheek when struck. Paul, the apostle of Christ, told the Roman Christians never to return evil for evil but to leave revenge to God.

How then can Christians allow themselves to get involved with such a thing as warfare?

This is a common question that's asked not just by pacifists; it's the question many thoughtful Christians are asking, especially as they try to come to grips with the lingering repercussions of the September 11, 2001, terrorist attacks on the United States, and with all that has happened on the heels of that tragedy.

The question, however, is far from new.

Although the earliest Christians did not worry so much about whether to get involved with warfare—mainly because they had little opportunity to do so in the Roman world of the first century—they did worry about how to account for the fact that Jesus was the Son of a God who ordered His people to kill and, on occasion, killed human beings Himself. This theological question troubled early Christians, and it's a theological question we also must wrestle with before we can begin to speak of a Christian doctrine of just war.

C. S. Lewis wrote in his preface to *Mere Christianity* that he wished "to explain and defend the belief that has been common to nearly all Christians at all times."[1] I wish to do much the same thing about Christian just war doctrine. The goal of this book is to present the traditional Christian just war doctrine in a clear, accessible manner that can be understood by anyone and offers Christians a helpful way to handle the moral problems of war. It's a doctrine many hundreds of years in the making, born and developed out of necessity as Christians lived in a world racked by recurrent war. The Christian just war doctrine is the best source for answers to the questions of *when* a war can be considered just and *how* such a war should be conducted.

In portraying the development of this doctrine, I rely a great deal upon two preeminent theologians in history, Thomas Aquinas from the thirteenth century and John Calvin from the sixteenth.

Why these two?

First (and most simply), Aquinas and Calvin are untainted by modern liberalism's distorted views of both religion and war and thus provide a useful Christian antidote to those distortions. Second (and more complicated), Aquinas and Calvin offer an approach to war that motivates Christians to be shaped morally and spiritually so they can act well on the battlefield and also in everyday life, which is something missing in almost every other modern perspective on war.

Aquinas and Calvin present an account of just war that is grounded in the character of God—the God who hates evil and restrains evildoers with acts of force, sometimes carried out through His children. In shaping Christians to be such people, the Church enables them to better cope with the nature of battle—as people who will bring appropriate restraint in the use of force against evil.

The plan of this book is simple. First, we'll take a quick look at the genesis of the Christian just war doctrine. We'll do this by exploring how some of the most revered figures in early Christianity grappled with the problem of how Christians should interact with the state and war.

In the second chapter we'll explore *why* the Christian tradition thinks it is important for Christians to get involved with warfare, and in the third chapter, we'll examine the relationship between Christian virtue and warfare, allowing leaders and soldiers to fight just wars justly. In these two chapters especially we rely on Calvin and Aquinas as our guides.

We then move on in chapters 4 and 5 to present what the Christian just war doctrine has concluded about *when* a war is just and *how* it can be justly fought.

In chapter 6 we'll examine three twentieth-century conflicts under the lenses of just war doctrine—World War II, the Vietnam conflict, and the Persian Gulf War—and then measure our nuclear arms policy against just war standards in chapter 7.

In the final chapter we'll discuss terrorism and examine how the just war tradition can help us deal with our contemporary situation.

CHAPTER ONE

Theologically Born

The Genesis of Christian Just War Doctrine

Traditional Christian teaching holds that some wars are worthy of Christian support and participation. Such wars are called "just" whenever true governing authorities (proper authority) have both a just cause and rightful intent in taking violent action. What counts as proper authority, a just cause, and rightful intent are all matters that, in theory, can be agreed upon by Christians and by governing authorities.

The Church was able to arrive at such an understanding because it had theological reasons for supposing some wars to be the kinds of causes Christians ought to support and encourage. These reasons were rooted in the character of God, especially as revealed in Old Testament Scripture.

This ethical and theological position started with the early Church Fathers such as Ambrose and Augustine. Centuries later, Thomas Aquinas built upon Augustine and formulated a theological position regarding war that, ideally at any rate, was to govern warfare. It greatly influenced European warfare in the Middle Ages, including the persistent religious strife of those centuries. This just war tradition was further articulated by Calvin and the Reformers and remained intact in the West, with little theological change, until the seventeenth century.

After that, as the West sought to shake itself loose from older ways of thinking (especially religious thinking) that seemed so prone to conflict, the emerging Enlightenment liberalism had little use for mixing theology with secular ethics. (In fact, liberalism's birth was in part a reaction against the brutal and fratricidal religious warfare of the late Middle Ages.) The Christian just war tradition came to be increasingly ignored by the West, with few exceptions, until the end of the First World War in the early twentieth century—when it became tragically apparent that war could use a little more restraint.

Unfortunately, by the time the West was again willing to pay attention to what the Church had to say about war, the message was muddled by two streams of theological thought that had sprung up in conflict with traditional Christian doctrine on this subject. One view was Christian pacifism, opposed to war in all cases. The other view—more recent but far broader in scope and far more pervasive in impact—was a so-called Christian "realism" (whose father was the famous Protestant theologian Reinhold Niebuhr) that allowed for evil means in the pursuit of a good cause. This consequentialism seeped so deeply into our culture that today it's hard for us to think about moral issues in any other way. In the realm of war, it means that in order to defeat an evil enemy and to save or protect our nation, we can do a few evil things ourselves. For Christians involved militarily, this amounts to suspending our sanctification while we do evil for the sake of good; we can later repent for such acts and return to an "ethically normal" life.

An odd thing to notice here is that both Christian pacifism and the Christian "realism" approach to war are in agreement about an essential point: Both assert that all use of force is evil and that the teachings of Christ forbid violence.

We'll have more to say in answer to these two alternative approaches later. For now, as we prepare to go back in time and survey how the Christian just war doctrine developed from the Church's earliest history until now, it's important to remember this fundamental distinction: The classic just war doctrine as articulated by the Church does *not* view all use of force as evil; rather, it declares that war can actually be a positive act of love entirely consistent with the character of God. Love of God and neighbor impels Christians to seek a just peace for all, especially for their neighbors, and military force is sometimes an appropriate means for seeking that peace.

WERE THE FIRST CHRISTIANS ALL PACIFISTS?

In the earliest centuries of the Church, is it true that most Christians were pacifist in their attitudes toward war? Was it only the rise of Constantine—Rome's first Christian emperor (A.D. 306–337)—that led to a fall from truth, making military participation and involvement with imperial Rome acceptable?

That's a common assumption. For example, in *Christian Attitudes Toward War and Peace,* Roland Bainton stated that "during this period no Christian author to our knowledge approved of Christian participation in battle."[1] John Howard Yoder, a leading pacifist scholar, has gone so far as to claim that Christians today cannot be faithful to the early Church unless they are pacifists.[2] Pacifist scholars tell us that early Christians rarely participated in the military, and the few who did were mainly bureaucrats who did not employ violence in their duties; the swords they carried were merely a symbol of administrative status. This predominant pacifism among early believers, Yoder says, was part of the Church's larger rejection of an inherently evil system—the empire and its Caesars.

Such a viewpoint is historically inaccurate and cannot be held with any integrity, given what we now know about early Christian practices.

Early generations of Christians were not active militarily because they had little chance to do otherwise. Roman authorities did not wish Christians in their ranks, and Christians generally were not eager to join. These early believers were not, for the most part, opponents of warfare and military service *per se;* instead, they objected to military service mainly because of the role of pagan religious practices in the military. Even with such objections, a divergence in Christian opinion existed, and Christian involvement in and support for military service grew steadily from the second century.[3]

We have little evidence that any early Church Father (besides Tertullian, who was later declared a heretic) held an unambiguously negative view of war. In fact, there's little evidence of *any* unified Christian attitude toward war during the earliest years of the Church era. It simply cannot be demonstrated that early Christians, in general, viewed either the military or the state as inherently evil, and hence completely off-limits to their participation.

In this chapter we'll survey the "founding fathers" of Christian just war doctrine. Although none of them actually presented the just war doctrine in a systematic way, they provided the necessary groundwork for the later "system builders" like Aquinas and Calvin.

FARMERS, SAILORS, SOLDIERS—EACH KNOWING GOD

Clement of Alexandria (A.D. 150–215) is one of the earliest Fathers to discuss warfare. Like most of the earliest Christian writers, Clement is hard to pin down on what exactly should be the Christian attitude toward war. He claimed that Christians should be trained in peace and not in war: "We do not train women like Amazons to be manly in war," he wrote, "since we wish even the men to be peaceable" (*The Teacher* I.12.98). In *Exhortation to the Greeks,* he called for an army of peace (XI.116-7); yet he also praised Moses as a military commander and showed a generally positive attitude toward war in Old Testament practices. Clement displayed a positive attitude toward soldiering in the New Testament as well. He claimed that Jesus, through the mouth of John the Baptist, commanded soldiers to be just but not to quit soldiering (Luke 3:14).

In one passage Clement seemed even to suggest that Christians as soldiers might be able to develop spiritually as much as believers in any other secular vocation. He first noted that as human beings it is our "very nature to be on intimate terms with God." As distinct from other living things, each human being "is truly a heavenly creature and…has been made for the vision of the heavens"; Clement therefore called upon each person "to come to a knowledge of God":

Laying hold of what is intimately and peculiarly his own as distinct from other living things, we advise him to outfit himself with godliness as an adequate preparation for his eternal journey. If you are a farmer, we say, till the earth, but acknowledge the God of farmers; if you love seafaring, sail on, but remember to call upon the celestial Helmsman. If you were in the army when you were seized by the knowledge of God, obey the Commander who gives just commands. (*Exhortation to the Greeks* X.100.2)

So farmers, sailors, and soldiers can all progress in spiritual relationship with God. Clement never hinted that the endeavors of the state, including military matters, are inherently at odds with Christianity.

FIGHTING THROUGH PRAYER

The Christian pacifism movement claims Origen (A.D. 185–254) as a hero, but it's hard to decide whether the term "pacifist" can truly and fairly be applied to him, at least in the way we think of it today. To modern ears, pacifism means the complete rejection of warfare as an inherently immoral practice. This was not Origen's view, though he was certainly opposed to Christians becoming soldiers.

The only work where Origen was concerned with Christian participation in warfare is the polemical *Contra Celsum*, written in response to a Roman philosopher named Celsus who had charged Christians with many crimes—spiritual, moral, social, and political. Attempting to counter the accusation from Celsus that Christians were not patriotic, Origen made an extraordinary argument. He said that all Christians should be given the same considerations as those in the pagan priesthood who were not required to give physical service in the military, but instead served the cause by praying for the emperor and the soldiers to triumph in battle.

> And, of course, in war time you do not enlist your priests. If this is a reasonable procedure, how much more so is it for Christians to fight as priests and worshipers of God while others fight as soldiers. Though they keep their right hands clean, the Christians fight through their prayers to God on behalf of those doing battle in a just cause and on behalf of an emperor who is ruling justly in order that all opposition and hostility toward those who are acting rightly may be eliminated. (VIII.73)

Moreover, Origen added, Christians supplied an irreplaceable aid to the emperor. By overcoming in prayer the very demons that cause wars, Christians actually help more than soldiers. So even though Christians did not go on campaign with the emperor, they did go to battle for him "by raising a special army of piety through our petitions to God" (VIII.73).

Elsewhere in this work, in discussing the life and activities of bees, Origen portrayed their life as a fitting lesson for human beings and declared that "if wars are ever necessary, they ought to be just and ordered" as the bees wage them (IV.82).

Nor did Origen judge the Roman system of government as inherently evil. In *Contra Celsum* he stated that Augustus, the founder of Rome's imperial administration, was providential for Christianity because the Pax Romana resulting from his reign provided a unity in the land that enabled Christianity to spread.

Origen's position, therefore, was decidedly *not* one of pure pacifism. He opposed military service for Christians, but he did not oppose war, and he suggested the acceptance of the just war. He did not reject violence but placed it in the hands of others; whatever force was needed for order and protection could be provided by Rome.

Origen viewed warfare as an activity that, if just, was something the Christian should participate in, even if only spiritually. The Christian first must pray against the very cause of warfare—the evil within human beings. Once the evil within manifests itself in the evil without, and peace and order are threatened, Christians have the duty to pray for the success of the Empire as partial payment of their debts toward their fellow citizens. God will respond to prayers in a just cause so that the unjust may be destroyed, as Christians combat the powers behind the threats to order and protection.

THE STATE LOOKS TO CHRISTIANS FOR HELP

Eusebius of Caesarea (A.D. 260–339) lived when Christians faced a new situation in the Church's history. For the first time, a Christian—Constantine—sat upon the Empire's throne, and public authorities were seeking Christian help in maintaining public order and justice.

It was easy for earlier Christians to shift onto others the burden for public security and order when society in general was suspicious of Christians, as the Romans were. But when society turned to Christians for help, it was quite another matter altogether.

In responding to these changed circumstances, Eusebius constructed a sacred history where earthly and heavenly things intermix, where the secular becomes a part of the spiritual, and where the heroic Christian can be either the holy Christian cleric or monk or the holy Christian warrior.

Eusebius viewed the Roman monarchy and the spread of the gospel as two blessings from God that together fulfilled Old Testament prophecies concerning universal peace and harmony. Eusebius went so far as to crown Constantine as a type of Christ who consummated a marriage of Church and Empire in a way unheard of before.

Eusebius saw, therefore, that the ordinary Christian should and must fight for the emperor, and he spoke of a Christian lifestyle that "lays down the practical rules for those fighting in a just war" (*Demonstration of the Gospel* I.8).

It's good at this point to remember that early Church writers typically conceived of the Christian moral life as a multilevel system with ordinary Christians on the bottom and a spiritual elite (monks, clerics, bishops) working their way to the top. The highest elite were not to participate physically in war but were to provide spiritual help for the military. Eusebius shared this perspective and reiterated that the spiritual elite must remain separated to some degree from the world—in praying for the emperor, rather than in fighting, just as Origen had insisted was the duty of all Christians.

In reference to less superior Christians who were "more concerned with human affairs" and who were "fighting in a just war," Eusebius stated that such individuals could attain "a secondary state of perfection which is suitable in its own way for their kind of life. Thus, no one is excluded from sharing in the Savior's coming" (*Demonstration of the Gospel* I.8).

Like Clement, Eusebius saw the ordinary Christian as being able to achieve some sort of Christian perfection while remaining in an earthly station, including a military station. Such a perfection was seen as secondary to the spiritual elite, but it was a real perfection nevertheless. Meanwhile the spiritual elite were to do the most good not by fighting for the emperor but by praying for him. There's even evidence that Eusebius was the first to propose a kind of military chaplaincy.

"EVEN IN THE MILITARY"

Basil (A.D. 329–379) was a follower of Origen, but in the wake of Eusebius he departed from Origen's teaching on Christian involvement in war. Basil distinguished between war and murder, but retained doubts about the propriety of killing in war:

> Our predecessors did not consider killing in war as
> murder but, as I understand it, made allowances for
> those who fought on the side of moderation and
> piety. Nonetheless, it is good to admonish those

whose hands are unclean to abstain just from communion for three years. (*Letter* 188.13)

It isn't clear what constituted "unclean hands" for Basil. He did not
say expressly that all bloodshed needed penance, which might indicate
that persons who did need it—those whose hands were "unclean"—
were those who did not fight "on the side of moderation and piety."
Such a view certainly accords with Basil's declaration elsewhere:

> I have become acquainted with a man who demon-
> strates that it is possible even in the military profes-
> sion to maintain perfect love for God, and that a
> Christian ought to be characterized not by the
> clothes he wears but by the disposition of his soul.
> (*Letter* 106)

No doubt the word *even* in this passage points to a general disenchantment with military pursuits, yet this disenchantment does
not forbid Christian participation in the military, and this separates
Basil from Origen.

So, by the time of Basil, even the more "pacifist" wing of the
Church as represented by followers of Origen was beginning to declare that Christians might participate in the military.

AN EMPEROR'S DUTY TO GOD

As we're beginning to see, the Christian just war doctrine was literally hundreds of years in the making, the product of thinking

from many illustrious Fathers of the Church. Though it did not spring forth, fully thought out, from the head of any one person, we might say nevertheless that it owes its origin primarily to one man—Ambrose of Milan (A.D. 339–397). The groundwork laid by Ambrose was followed by Augustine, then by Aquinas, then by Reformation Fathers such as Calvin.

Ambrose's understanding of the state (or, as the modern ethicist would say, his political theology) gives us the proper context for accurately understanding his view of soldiering and warfare as he led the way to more active participation by Christians in the secular world.

Ambrose held a high government office before becoming a bishop, and he knew that political order was necessary for ensuring community life. Following the teaching of Paul (Romans 13:1-7), he held that government is a divine institution, and as such it facilitates mutual help among citizens—"Man was made for the sake of man," Ambrose claimed (*On Duties* 1.134, 135). We may therefore expect the emperor and those in his service (soldiers) to have a divine duty to preserve the order which facilitates our life together, an order which includes the Church.

How this works out in actual practice can be seen in Ambrose's correspondence with the emperors of his day.

In a letter to the emperor Valentinian, Ambrose said that the emperor's duty to the state (including his use of the sword) is a duty to God and is therefore under the Church (*Epistle* 17). This is key, because if responsibility for using the sword is under the Church, then distinctly Christian morals will govern how that sword is to be used in practice.

Highly revealing of this line of thought is a later letter from Ambrose to the emperor Theodosius (*Epistle* 51) following a massacre of Thessalonian citizens by imperial forces. In A.D. 390, the people of Thessalonica rioted against an army garrison and killed its commander. The government's reprisal was the slaughter of seven thousand people who were attending an exhibition. Ambrose wrote to the emperor and ordered him to do penance for this action.

Holding up King David as an example for good rulers to follow, Ambrose warned Theodosius that only "by humbling his soul before God" could this sin that blighted the Empire be removed. He further urged Theodosius to repent of other misdeeds and to "conquer by love of duty" his "natural impetuosity." Should Theodosius refuse to repent, Ambrose threatened to not "offer the Holy Sacrifice" in church while the emperor was present.

Throughout this letter, Ambrose likened himself to a rod of authority over the emperor, offering useful advice, correction, threats, and spiritual consolation. In response, Theodosius submitted to Ambrose and did penance for his sins. In doing so, the emperor acknowledged his responsibility within the Church for the proper use of his sword.

For Ambrose, the state does not have a completely free rein in how it preserves civil order but is under the Church's guidance to some degree. Furthermore, the state is successful in preserving civil order only insofar as God makes it possible. The state, therefore, cannot ignore the Church's guidance and advice on the proper maintenance of civil order without ignoring the very power behind its success and victories.

WARRIORS IN SCRIPTURE

When the emperor Gratian requested Ambrose to write him a treatise proving the divinity of Jesus Christ, Ambrose responded with the first two books of what became a five-book work, *On Faith*. In it, Ambrose began by praising the emperor for his eagerness for instruction on the very eve of his departure to war and urged him to go forth to victory as a layman of the Church, protected by the shield of faith and carrying the sword of the Spirit.

Ambrose recorded his words of prayer for the military and the emperor: "No military eagles, no flight of birds, here lead the van of our army, but Thy Name, Lord Jesus, and Thy worship" (*On Faith* 2.142). He prayed, "Show forth now a plain sign of Thy Majesty" so that Gratian, "upheld by the aid of Thy Might Supreme...might win the prize of victory for his faith" (2.143). In these passages Ambrose brought a number of distinctively Christian characteristics to warfare and soldiering. The name and the worship of the Christian God goes forth for the army, thus making victory over the enemy possible. God is with the emperor so long as the Church is on his side.

And how are the emperor, his commanders, and plain soldiers to act in battle? What kind of behavior befits a warrior who serves under a Christian emperor, and what befits a soldier or commander who is also a Christian himself? Ambrose did not discuss these matters in a direct way, but he did discuss military virtues at length. From these discussions we can glean an idea of how the Christian soldier is to behave in battle, and more important, *why* he does so.

The Bible, for Ambrose, was the supreme authority for guidance in action. It was largely from Scripture—the record of the "fathers"—that Ambrose found guidance in shaping the moral life of the virtuous person. In a revealing passage he noted that his work *On Duties* offered readers "a large number of examples... drawn from our forefathers, and also many words of theirs," and that these "offer much instruction" (3.138).

These biblical examples were to be followed, not just talked about. "Let the life of the fathers be for us a mirror of virtue, not a mere collection of shrewd and clever acts. Let us show reverence in following them, not mere cleverness in discussing them" (1.116).

One common characteristic Ambrose found among the Old Testament Fathers is the virtue of courage—especially courage shown in battle. His discussions of Old Testament figures were filled with praise for their military virtues displayed in fitting situations. "How brave was Joshua," Ambrose exclaimed, "who in one battle laid low five kings together with their people" (1.205; Joshua 10).

In the eyes of Ambrose, King David was *the* just warrior. David was "brave in battle, patient in adversity, peaceful in Jerusalem, and merciful in victory" (1.114). To Ambrose, there appeared to be no virtue lacking in Israel's shepherd-king. David considered not his own advantage but the advantage of his people. He "never waged war unless driven to it. Thus prudence was combined in him with fortitude in battle." And David "never entered on a war without seeking counsel of the Lord" (1.177). In common with other Old Testament figures, David possessed "fortitude, which both in warfare and at home is conspicuous in greatness of mind and distinguishes itself in the strength of the body" (1.115).

WHEN LOVE DEMANDS FORCE

The key to Ambrose's approach to war's morality rests with his view of how virtue works in the virtuous person. Ambrose stated that there's never a conflict between virtue and expediency, and that, therefore, the virtuous should always aim for right moral action.

Ambrose pointed to love ("charity") as the highest virtue: "Charity is perfect," he wrote; "it is the fulfilling of the law" (*Epistle* 29). This love enhances the virtue of justice because it eliminates motives of self-interest that can easily contaminate just acts. The same is true for the virtue of courage—it operates under the guidance of love in order to prevent self-interest from corrupting courageous acts.

What this means for the soldier can be seen in Ambrose's discussion of John the Baptist's conversation with soldiers, men who must display courage on a regular basis in order to act well in their duties. Ambrose concentrated on the part mercy played in John the Baptist's advice ("Rob no one by violence or by false accusation, and be content with your wages"—Luke 3:14) and argued that mercy is a perfect form of virtue for the soldier because all the soldier does can be described as acts of mercy for the common good (*Discourses on Luke* 1.77).

The emphasis Ambrose placed on mercy in the soldier's duty is striking. Mercy was singled out among the virtues as that quality in the soldier that is most befitting in his duties. We can almost say that, for Ambrose, soldiering was an office of mercy and charity.

It's important to emphasize that Ambrose was not twisting

the logic of the concept of love in order to make allowances for the use of force. No Church Father before Ambrose conceived of love in this way, but we find Ambrose articulating love as the motivating force behind the Christian's use of force. Ambrose expanded on this in such a way that the use of force becomes a positive duty, and the failure to use force when it is fitting becomes a lack of love. In Ambrose's eyes, the Christian who stands idly by while his neighbor is attacked is no virtuous person, and perhaps not even a Christian.

We have Moses as an example, Ambrose said, in using force to protect our neighbor; when Moses came to the aid of his neighbor who was "receiving hard treatment at the hands of an Egyptian, he defended him" and "gave this as a first proof of his fortitude in war" (*On Duties* 1.179).

The Christian can use violence when he occupies an office that calls for it. Such Christians respond to violence from enemies who threaten peace and order, and they do so not passively but with force.

When Ambrose discussed how love governs justice, he again gave Moses as an example of how this works. The example, revealingly, is one of war:

> Thus holy Moses, feared not to undertake terrible
> wars for his people's sake, nor was he afraid of the
> arms of the mightiest kings, nor yet was he
> frightened at the savagery of barbarian nations.
> He put to one side the thought of his own safety
> so as to give freedom to the people (*On Duties*
> 1.135).

Love, in this context, does not merely allow for the use of force; it demands the use of force. Moses was afraid *not* to use force for the sake of his people.

Therefore the virtuous soldier—whose duty it is to protect others—is just that person who fulfills the duty to defend the neighbor at risk. "The law of courage," claimed Ambrose, is exercised "in driving away all harm" (*On Duties* 1.179). Here the very duty of civil courage is to protect the weak from injury.

Just as the duty of the soldier is to protect the empire with force, the duty of the clergy, Ambrose said, is to pray for the success of that force. And both the soldiers who fight and the clergy who pray for victory are to do this for the sake of others.

Ambrose held that soldiering was forbidden to no one except clergy. And no one, except soldiers and other private citizens acting for the interests of others, should take another's life.[4]

Ambrose's views on warfare and the use of force represent a change in the Christian tradition, but it is a change achieved *within* the tradition. Ambrose did not split with earlier Church Fathers, nor did he radically compromise the tradition he received from them. Instead, he expanded on the moral vocabulary handed down to him in a way that expanded the tradition's scope. In other words, what Ambrose does with charity in no way contradicts what earlier Church Fathers had taught.

Christians fight in the army and pray for victory because they are formed by the perfect virtue of charity. For Ambrose, the ruling virtue in the moral life was love—as it also would be for Augustine, for Aquinas, and for Calvin.

BECAUSE OF SIN

What Augustine (A.D. 354–430) bequeathed to the Christian doctrine of just war was a clear understanding that human sin makes necessary the use of force.

Augustine did not view war in terms of the dangers to material interests or even to human survival. Instead, for him the wrongness of war lay in the moral evil of disordered desire and twisted inward dispositions.

The emphasis Augustine placed on our inward disposition toward evil cannot be overstated. The basic assumption in Augustine's thought was original sin: Adam's fall tainted the entire human race; humanity is a "mass of sin" inherently at odds with God and under just condemnation (*City of God* XXI.10).

Humanity's essential goal is to bring itself into right relation with God, to seek its proper place in the divine order. This, in fact, is what proper Christian behavior is all about. But only a correct inward disposition can place a person in the right relation to God, a disposition shaped and informed by the love of God.

Because human beings are so tainted by original sin and by the resulting lust for domination, humanity is never going to improve appreciably from a moral perspective. Dealing with humanity's "mass of sin"—holding its evil actions in check—is therefore the continuing purpose for the earthly "city," the governmental community such as the state. The state is formed to hold evil actions in check by minimizing disorder and chaos, thus providing liberty and safety for its citizens to reach their ultimate good of right relation with God. The Christian as well as the pagan benefits from this protection of order.

Augustine did not intend, however, to give the state carte blanche on how it performs its task of checking disorder and providing liberty and security. As rulers carry out their duty to "direct and protect the state," Augustine required them to put their power in the service of God. This can be summarized as three basic duties for rulers: to provide a place for the worship of God, to carry out their judicial tasks, and to take vengeance on wrongdoers. To succeed in all three of these duties, the establishment of peace and order is essential.

Augustine viewed peace as humanity's most fundamental need. Peace therefore is always the end goal in war, just as doing good is always the goal in human actions; what prevents the doing of good is not war, but the malice in human hearts—a lack of love.

Because peace is the ultimate goal of war, the peacemaker who uses the word is better than the peacemaker who uses the sword. Nevertheless, when the word and prayer fail, violent action must be taken. The goal is always peace—preferably by the word, but if not, then by the sword.

For Augustine, choosing to go to war was never a choice between two evils. We're never to do evil in order that good may come,[5] so war can never be the choice of a lesser evil. Justified violence for Augustine was something demanded partly for the sake of justice and peace, and ultimately for the sake of love.

For the Christian, a love-informed disposition guides our right actions, and this disposition sometimes demands acts of violence. All "just" violence is the product of this love-informed disposition that seeks the good. War, therefore, is not something evil for

Christians, nor even a necessary evil; the use of just force is a virtuous act demanded by love, a positive good to be practiced and pursued by the virtuous.

And although war among fallen humanity is inevitable, and no one is secure from war, yet under God's providence everything—including war—works for the good.

With Augustine's contributions building on the foundation laid by Ambrose and other Church Fathers, everything is now in place for the system builders—Aquinas and Calvin—to refine the Christian doctrine of just war.

CHAPTER TWO

Why Christians Use Force

What God's Character Tells Us

Christians from the very beginning have asked the question, "How can the God who tells us to love our enemies and to turn the other cheek be the same God who orders His people to make war and to kill?"

How can Christians reconcile God the Warrior with God the Crucified?

This theological question is also a question of character—God's character. Christians believe they can have some understanding of the character of God because He has revealed Himself through Holy Scripture. The Bible is an accurate account of how God has acted in history in His dealings with His people, and those actions accurately reveal what He is like.

What then does the Bible tell us about God in regard to war and violence?

GOD AS WARRIOR

The Old Testament reveals that God is just, merciful, and loving; it also reveals that God has a warlike character. "The LORD is…a dread warrior" declared Jeremiah (20:11). The prophet Zephaniah declared that the Lord is "a warrior who gives victory" (3:17). God is often referred to as "The LORD of hosts"—a commander of great armies.

God demonstrates warlike characteristics throughout the Old Testament, in a multitude of instances. In Judges, to choose one book, God fights through human beings in human conflict; here we find God positively saying yes to human warfare. In the Psalms, to choose another book, David declared that the Lord is "strong and mighty, the LORD, mighty in battle" (24:8), and he insisted that God "trains my hands for war" (18:34).

God as Warrior is not peripheral here but one of the major characteristics of God as presented in the Hebrew Scriptures.

PACIFIST ARGUMENTS

People who are uncomfortable with the Old Testament's teaching about war usually employ an "evolutionary" understanding of the Old Testament as they try to reconcile the Old Testament's Warrior God with the New Testament's God of peace and love. They typically view the concept of "God the Warrior" as a "primitive" perspective that would later be abandoned in more enlightened times. (This evolutionary theory should not be confused with progressive revelation. Progressive revelation does not cancel out what comes before; it only helps us to understand previous revelation better.) Evolutionary theories generally come from those who view the person and preaching of Christ in isolation from the rest of Scripture.

Many pacifists, and those influenced by their arguments, have argued that Jesus represents, if not a new God, then at least a new approach by God to His creation in comparison with the Old Testament. Whereas God used to deal violently with His creation, now He uses the peace and love exemplified by the character of Jesus.

Another pacifist approach is to try to find a prevailing pacifist message even in the Old Testament. Theologian Millard Lind argues for this perspective in *Yahweh Is a Warrior: The Theology of Warfare in Ancient Israel.*[1] But Lind's book is entirely unconvincing to one informed by the likes of Augustine, Aquinas, Luther, and Calvin, and it's unlikely anyone who isn't already a pacifist would interpret Scripture the way Lind does.

Lind's main argument is that Yahweh fought for His people by miracle and not "by sword and spear." For Lind, this means Israel had to rely upon God rather than on human soldiers and weapons for victory in battle. On this account, the human agent in the work of war is more a prophet and executioner than a soldier. However, executioners still execute, and even Lind finally concedes that, even if we minimize the importance of human fighting in the face of God's victory-giving power, human beings did fight by God's command and approval.[2]

Moreover, Lind doesn't address many portions of Scripture that pose problems for his thesis. To take one notable example, he makes nothing of the story in the book of Joshua (10:12-27) where God held the sun in place so Israel could continue to fight, kill, and win.

A more balanced and convincing treatment of warfare in the Old Testament is T. R. Hobbs's *A Time for War,* which argues that "there is no evidence to suggest that warfare *per se* is regarded as even a necessary evil."[3] According to Hobbs, Lind's thesis suffers from the fallacy of reading back into the past the perspectives of the present—in Lind's case, radical pacifism. True, the prophets sometimes criticized the wars of the monarchy, but the evidence suggests that the prophets objected not to war *per se* but to warfare as a tool of imperial expansion. The problem they addressed was one of the misuse of power and not of war.

Furthermore, to note that Israel had Yahweh to fight miraculously for them is not to condemn all human involvement in war, but to talk about a certain kind of warfare. The story of Gideon, for example, demonstrates the relative unimportance of human strength and numbers in carrying out God's plans for destroying an enemy of Israel, but Gideon and a small number of men did fight and kill. The account of their deeds does not frown upon the use of violence but gives us an example of a God-directed, "limited, but real use of violence."[4]

We must face theological and biblical facts. God's warlike characteristics cannot be "spiritualized away" in an effort to deny the name "God the Warrior" in favor of a new name "God the Pacifist."

Of course, I'm not denying a spiritual sense to Scripture; "God the Warrior" certainly can take on more meanings than God leading His people to material victory. But the spiritual sense of Scripture cannot eliminate the literal sense. God's warlike characteristics are so much a part of His character as drawn by the Old Testament writers and compilers that to reject these characteristics is to reject the God of the Old Testament.

THE UNITY OF THE TESTAMENTS

God certainly demonstrates a warlike character in the Old Testament, but can we say the same about Him in the New Testament?

The relationship between the two Testaments tells us something about the character of God and hence how to set some parameters around acceptable ways of interpreting the life and work of Christ. Let's make a few quick points.

It should first be noted that for those living in the New Testament world, the issue was not whether the Old Testament was sufficiently Christian but whether the emerging New Testament was sufficiently biblical. Christ was and is the key to reading the entire biblical witness in the right way, yet Jesus Himself draws our attention to the Old Testament witness, and as such, "he cannot impose on it an interpretation that it resists," as Old Testament scholar John Goldingay rightly insists.[5] The New Testament, Goldingay argues, "presupposes the theological and moral foundation laid by the Old Testament."[6]

We can fully understand Christ and the New Testament only against the background of the Old Testament's broader concerns, and we cannot interpret the character of Jesus in a way that conflicts with God's eternal and unchanging moral character as it is revealed in the Old Testament. The character of Jesus must harmonize with the portrayal of God in the Old Testament. The New Testament reveals a new covenant but not a new God.

Nor can we say that God's warlike characteristics cannot be found in Christ, for we cannot deny the obvious: The Son of God is *God.* This is one of the ground rules for how we interpret the life and work of Christ. And we must in fact remember that God's warlike character receives renewed emphasis at the end of history as told in the New Testament book of Revelation.

There is, of course, more than one way to interpret the life and work of Jesus Christ, and the tradition represented by figures such as Ambrose, Augustine, Aquinas, Luther, and Calvin is by no means agreed on all points. Nevertheless, they agreed on enough of the essential points of the story that we can, indeed, talk about a single traditional approach to interpreting the life and work of Christ. This classical approach assumes a unity between the God of the Old Testament and the God of the New, and part of its goal is to understand the person and work of Christ in light of that unity.

In maintaining the moral and theological continuity between the Old Testament and the New Testament, the classical Christian tradition rejects outright the idea that Jesus was correcting or making a more spiritual religion in the New Testament or that Christianity's moral precepts are not those of the Old Testament. Aquinas reminded us, for example, that in regard to moral precepts, the New Law adds nothing to the Old Law as regards external action—regarding "ethics," we might say.

The evolutionary understanding of Old Testament faith not only fails to match Old Testament data and do justice to the history of Israel, but it also contradicts this classical Christian tradition. To disallow God as Warrior is to join with ancient heresies that held that the God of the Old Testament was not the God of the New Testament and that none of the Old Testament's warlike imagery of God applies to Jesus. Christians err when they relegate God's warlike characteristics to obsolescence, when they ignore those characteristics, or when they make them of no consequence to the Christian's moral life.

ROMANS AT THE CENTER

The key to this traditional Christian approach is to follow Ambrose, Augustine, Aquinas, Luther, and Calvin in looking at Jesus Christ through Paul's letter to the Romans. When we place Paul's letter to the Romans in the center of Scripture, Christ's character becomes much clearer to us. Romans is the key text for understanding both Christ and governmental authority and responsibility.

We'll be looking at Romans with Calvin as our guide. I could have chosen Augustine, Aquinas, or Luther, but Calvin is the most helpful for this book's purposes because he was always mindful of

Anabaptist radicals who insisted on complete pacifism. The Anabaptists of Calvin's day were fond of arguing that the two testament periods were totally different, especially when it comes to God's relationship with His people. For the Anabaptists, the Old Testament moral law was for the Jews alone and had no authority for Christians.

Calvin's opponents made no distinction for Christians between the authority of the Old Testament moral law and that of Old Testament ceremonial Law: Both had passed away, they said. Christians need to live by the moral precepts of the New Testament, which supersede those found in the Old Testament. For the Anabaptists, the Old Testament was all outdated "Law" with no "gospel."

Calvin found his Anabaptist opponents dangerously close to the gnostic heresy found in the writings of the ancient heretics Marcion and Mani. When Calvin took up the task of refuting the Anabaptists, he drew heavily upon a work by Augustine called *Against Faustus the Manichaean*. Faustus was a notable Manichaean who argued in good gnostic fashion that the God of the Old Testament was not the God of the New Testament. Manichaeans believed that the God of the Old Testament was an evil god who created the evil material world. Jesus was the true God who came to save human beings from the evil of the material world. The gnostics pointed out that while the God of the Jews ordered them to make war, Jesus tells His followers to turn the other cheek when struck. Calvin found the Anabaptists of his day using the same sort of arguments.

OUT OF JUSTICE, MERCY, AND LOVE

What is the God of the Old Testament really like, when we take in the fullest picture?

When Calvin searched for the knowledge we can have of God from Hebrew Scripture, he found especially helpful the passage in Exodus (34:6-7) in which God is named "Jehovah, a merciful and gracious God, patient and of much compassion…in whose presence the innocent will not be innocent and who visitest the iniquity of the fathers upon the children and the children's children" (*Institutes* I.10.2). For Calvin, this passage was the clearest and most comprehensive summation of God's characteristics, or as he put it, God's "powers." God is known particularly by His kindness, goodness, mercy, justice, judgment, and truth.

Through the prophet Jeremiah we're given a similar yet even more concise description of God's character. God tells Jeremiah that He is the Lord who exercises "mercy, judgment, and justice in the earth" (9:24, Calvin's Latin translation). Calvin insisted that we cannot understand any of these powers apart from the others. Mercy, judgment, and justice are each a part of God's revealed character, and one never supersedes the other. This tells us that God's use of force can never be disconnected from His justice, judgment, and mercy.

For Calvin (as well as for Aquinas), God's warlike characteristics (exemplified particularly by His wrath) could be understood in a more excellent and higher way only by realizing that they're always intermingled with His characteristics of justice, mercy, and love. When we read that God is a Warrior, we should understand this as a subset of God the Just, Merciful, and Loving.

A close look at God's warlike character in the Old Testament confirms this critically important fact: His use of force, whether by His own hand or the hands of His creatures, is always a product of His justice, mercy, and love. In fact, we may say that God has warlike characteristics *because* He is just, merciful, and loving.

These characteristics remind us that God always gives us nothing less than what we deserve, but frequently more—which emphasizes both His justice and His mercy. The very fact that God would show us mercy—so much mercy, in fact, that He sent His son to die for us—emphasizes His love.

There are certainly more characteristics of God than justice, mercy, and love, but I believe that these capture the most notable characteristics of God in a summary form, insofar as anything can. God is the ultimate loving, faithful, and merciful being.

And this says something about how Christians should view our use of force today. Because we know why and how to use force only by knowing why and how God uses force, our acts of force must spring from and be guarded by the virtues of justice, mercy, and love.

LAW AND GOSPEL IN HARMONY

Calvin also insisted on the traditional Christian position regarding the relationship of the two Testaments: There is no conflict between law and gospel. Christ brought not a new law but His

Spirit to renew our hearts so that we would want to obey and please God, and the only way we can obey and please Him is to follow His moral law, which we can do by the grace of the Holy Spirit.

Against the Anabaptists, Calvin insisted that the love command of the gospel (love your neighbor as yourself) is wholly consonant with the Ten Commandments (the very summation of God's moral law for human beings). So the Sermon on the Mount is not a code of perfection for the few (the Anabaptists argued that only the few who withdraw from the world can follow it) but God's guidance for all who live in the world.

Two of the main lessons Calvin drew from the Sermon on the Mount are that a disciple of Christ must never seek personal vengeance and that charity (love of God) and justice are one. Perfect love never sacrifices *justice,* though Christians may sacrifice *their own rights* for the sake of love.

WHAT CALVIN DISCOVERED IN ROMANS

Calvin was able to make these formulations once he had made his way through Paul's letter to the Romans—especially the twelfth and thirteenth chapters.

Romans 12 contains Paul's practical advice to his audience after all the theological arguments that have made up the bulk of the letter. In the letter's preceding chapters, Paul argued that the righteousness of God is to be sought from God alone, that salvation comes from God's mercy alone, and that all blessings come from Christ alone. Thus Christians get their righteousness, salvation, and mercy from God and from no one else. This is who Christians are—people totally dependent upon God. *How should these people act in the world?* That's the question Paul answered in the remaining chapters of the letter.

The first two verses of chapter 12 set the stage for all the moral advice that follows:

> I appeal to you therefore, brethren, by the mercies
> of God, to present your bodies as a living sacrifice,
> holy and acceptable to God, which is your spiritual
> worship. Do not be conformed to this world but be
> transformed by the renewal of your mind, that you
> may prove what is the will of God, what is good
> and acceptable and perfect.

In these opening verses Paul stressed the Christian's commitment to and dependence upon God as the foundation for morally correct behavior. This governs everything that follows—including Paul's advice about how Christians are to relate to the governing authorities.

Paul's word to Christians in Romans 13:1-7 has been the traditional cornerstone of all Christian teaching on our obligations toward the state. Before discussing it, let's get it before us:

> Let every person be subject to the governing
> authorities. For there is no authority except from

God, and those that exist have been instituted by God. Therefore he who resists the authorities resists what God has appointed, and those who resist will incur judgment. For rulers are not a terror to good conduct, but to bad. Would you have no fear of him who is in authority? Then do what is good, and you will receive his approval, for he is God's servant for your good. But if you do wrong, be afraid, for he does not bear the sword in vain; he is the servant of God to execute his wrath on the wrongdoer. Therefore one must be subject, not only to avoid God's wrath but also for the sake of conscience. For the same reason you also pay taxes, for the authorities are ministers of God, attending to this very thing. Pay all of them their dues, taxes to whom taxes are due, revenue to whom revenue is due, respect to whom respect is due, honor to whom honor is due.

The most important point of the passage is that all earthly political authority is given by God. This means that all earthly powers are subject to the limits God places on their authority. Powers that exceed their authority will have to answer to God, as will those powers that fail to do what they're supposed to do— reward and protect the good and punish the evil.

The second important point from this passage is that earthly authority is an agent of God's wrath. God's wrath and judgment on evildoers are usually worked through the human political order. Thus, Paul tells us in effect that the soldier (or policeman—there was little distinction between the two in ancient times, as both were military jobs) is an agent of God's wrath.

It's important, however, not to lose sight of what we've said earlier: God's wrath is always encompassed by God's love. The soldier is as much an agent of God's love as of His wrath, for the two characteristics are harmonious in God. As Calvin argues, "Paul meant to refer the precept of respecting power of the magistrates to the law of love" (*Commentary on Romans* 13:17).

NO PERSONAL VENGEANCE

Just before his comments concerning the governing authorities, Paul exhorted his readers to "repay no one evil for evil, but take thought for what is noble in the sight of all. If possible, so far as it depends upon you, live peaceably with all. Beloved, never avenge yourselves, but leave it to the wrath of God" (Romans 12:17-19).

The key here is the phrase, "so far as it depends upon you." Paul realized that peace does not always lie with us. We must bear much for the sake of peace, but Calvin rightly argued that when peace is no longer possible, we must be ready "to fight courageously" (*Commentary on Romans* 12:18).

The just soldier does not repay evil for evil when he uses force justly, for a just use of force is no evil. By using force justly, he does what is "noble in the sight of all." The just soldier does not act in personal vengeance but is an agent of God's vengeance. Soldiers carry the sword to execute God's wrath, which is in harmony with His love, and that's exactly what they do when they use their swords in just warfare. For the Christian, soldiering is an office of love and as such can brook no motives of personal vengeance.

AS IMMORAL AS PROSTITUTION?

With our exegesis of Romans in hand we can now, with further help from Calvin, turn to the Gospels and finally the Old Testament with the purpose of understanding better how the just use of force is a God-like act fully pleasing to God.

One place in Scripture that just war defenders like to point to is the passage in Luke, mentioned earlier, where John the Baptist gave advice to soldiers. Why did John fail to tell the soldiers to quit their profession? If the use of force is inherently immoral and a particular profession requires the use of force, then that profession is immoral. On the pacifist view, soldiering is on the same moral plane as prostitution. If there's no moral difference between soldiering and prostitution (and pacifists must hold this proposition), we would expect John to warn any soldier who came to him to quit soldiering, just as we would expect him to warn any prostitute who came to him to quit prostitution. Can you imagine John giving advice to prostitutes about how to prostitute more justly? Yet he did advise soldiers on how to soldier more justly. What's going on here?

Calvin reminded us that John's very purpose was "to make ready a people prepared for the Lord" (*Commentary on Luke* 3:14), and that the advice he gave to those he baptized was consonant with that purpose. Thus John advised the soldiers to use their power justly, and not to give it up entirely, for to do so would mean that Christ destroys "what his heavenly Father sanctioned." Calvin added that a Christian who desires to soldier must be drawn to that profession by a regard for public advantage, emphasizing further the idea that the Christian soldier uses force out of love of neighbor.

CALVIN'S VIEW ON PASSAGES THE PACIFISTS LIKE

One event in Scripture that pacifists like to point to is Jesus' temptation in the desert (Matthew 4:5-11; Mark 1:13; Luke 4:5-13). Pacifists make much of Satan's offer to give Jesus the kingdoms of the earth if Jesus would bow down to Satan.

We know from Romans, however, that all power is from God, so we see Jesus' temptation as an appeal to seek the kingdoms of the world in another manner than from His Father. Calvin said Jesus was tempted here to "rob God of the government of the world and to claim it for himself" (*Commentary on Matthew* 4:5-11).

Satan could not deliver to Jesus what he promised. Satan could not make Jesus a present of the kingdoms of the world without Jesus cooperating with him (and possibly not even then; Satan, as we know, is the "father of lies").

As I said before, pacifists also like to make much of Jesus' advice to "turn the other cheek" when struck (Matthew 5:38-41; Luke 6:29-30). But this passage becomes clear when we stop trying to interpret one small portion of Scripture without regard for the whole. For Calvin, the passage was "best interpreted" by Paul, who enjoined us to overcome evil with good and to forgo personal vengeance. Thus we see—along with Ambrose, Augustine, Aquinas, and Luther—that Jesus' goal is to restrain *personal* retaliation, not to restrain political force, which is, after all, an agent of His Father's wrath and love.

LOOKING AGAIN AT THE OLD TESTAMENT

With Paul as our guide we now have a way of interpreting the Old Testament, and a way of finding Christ there. For Calvin, the Old Testament no less than the New has given us knowledge of God. In this regard the Old Testament is in no way inferior to the New, for God did not change His character when He took on human flesh. Christ's coming changed nothing about the just use of force, for such use of force is consonant with God's eternal character.

Calvin argued that the differences between the two Testaments are to be found in the degree of clarity of revelation. *What* is revealed—Jesus Christ—remains constant in both. Christians are in the same position as the Old Testament believers—waiting for the fulfillment of God's promise. According to Calvin, the gospel does not introduce a new method of salvation; rather, it confirms the Law and proves the fulfillment of it: "What was shadow," the gospel "has made substance" (*Institutes* II.9.4).

For Calvin, the character of God and Christ is reflected throughout the Old Testament. Let's look at two places where he saw this: the books of Joshua and Isaiah.

In the book of Joshua, Christ appears as a divine warrior. He appears to Joshua in order to encourage him before a great battle. We know this is no mere angel, for Joshua is ordered to remove his sandals, just as Moses was warned beside the burning bush.

Throughout the book of Joshua we find God exerting His own might in the swords of His chosen people. On occasion, as when He sent hail upon His enemies, God did the killing Himself. God even held the sun in place at one point in the story so that the killing could continue (10:13).

One of the striking things about Joshua's battles—and one of the most repellent things to modern eyes—is the extermination of whole peoples. As Calvin noted, "Clemency is justly praised as one of the principal virtues; but it is the clemency of those who moderate their wrath" (*Commentary on Joshua* 10:40). Joshua, however, was not a wrathful warrior; like all just warriors, he was the instrument of God's wrath, and God's wrath is always consonant with His love, even if we cannot see it.

We also find God the Crucified in the Old Testament, particularly in Isaiah's "Suffering Servant" passage (52:13–53:12). Here we see that God's love for human beings prompts Him to send His own Son, so that God might bear away our guilt before Him. Yet we cannot lose sight of God's wrath even here. We cannot lose sight of what the Suffering Servant does later on in the story. God who is crucified is also God whose sword will execute judgment, "and those slain by the LORD shall be many" (Isaiah 66:16). The victors, according to Isaiah, will gaze upon the dead bodies of all those who transgressed against God.

We must conclude, therefore, that God's redemption and wrath are both in harmony with His love. We go wrong when we emphasize one at the expense of the other. God's loving redemption continues to operate in the form of His Church that beckons all to enter into fellowship with Him. Meanwhile, God's loving wrath also continues to operate—in the form of earthly political order that promotes virtue, punishes vice, and fights just wars justly for the sake of its citizens whose care God has entrusted to it.

THE STATE AND THE CHARACTER OF GOD

God's character is reflected in earthly political structures, and this should tell us something about how such structures should rule and wage war. Calvin—along with Aquinas—followed an Aristotelian line of thinking in claiming that God made human beings as political animals. Organized society was not the result of sin, and politics *per se* does not presuppose violence.

Post-Fall politics, unfortunately, *does* presuppose violence. After the fall of humanity, war is a constant, a fact of human politics. War therefore is a part of life, and all life is to be lived before God.

We get a hint at what this means for us in the book of Deuteronomy, where war is an accepted fact, but God "controls, circumscribes, directs and harnesses it" to His purposes, as John

Goldingay notes.[7] War is yoked to a moral purpose. Thus war, though a result of sin, is not necessarily evil itself—just as police action is the result of sin but is not necessarily evil itself.

For Calvin, civil government is one of those external means by which God invites us into the fellowship of Jesus and holds us therein. (The Holy Spirit is the internal means for doing this.) Civil government—especially the force it uses to protect order and promote good—makes our life together as human beings possible. Calvin argued that those who would take away political order— and the means by which it is kept—would take away our "very humanity" (*Institutes* IV.20.2). Those who revile coercion revile God Himself.

Calvin pointed out that the Anabaptists claimed a perfection that can no longer exist this side of history—a politics without violence. In his *Commentary on Micah,* Calvin remarked that the Anabaptist political scheme would be ideal if fallen human beings were angels (4:3).

For Calvin and Aquinas, any theory concerning nonviolent politics must be a thought experiment about a kind of politics that may have existed before the fall of humanity or one that might exist after Armageddon. Politics is not inherently violent; we can imagine a nonviolent politics because we were made by God to inhabit such a world. Unfortunately, we made a mess of things and precluded any further chances in this world of a politics without violence. Because of our fallen nature, nonviolent political associations are now inherently impossible for human beings to achieve. In principle, all politics now presupposes violence.

Earthly rulership is a divine ordinance and one that makes being a good human being possible. Civil authority is thus a holy and lawful calling before God and is, in fact, among the most sacred and most honorable of all callings that can come to human beings. Magistrates serve God in a most holy office, for they are actually God's deputies. Virtuous soldiering is a part of this holy office, which allowed Calvin to make such strong claims as to say that a Christian called to serve his country "doth not offend God in going to the wars, but is in a holy vocation, which cannot be reproved without blaspheming of God" (*Short Instruction* 78). Soldiering in a just war is a "holy vocation," and those who reprove such soldiers are actually guilty of blasphemy.

Why is just soldiering a holy vocation? And why are those who reprove just soldiers guilty of blasphemy? The answers are connected. Just soldiering is holy because those who justly restrain evil are acting in a God-like fashion. Just soldiering, in this view, is consonant with holy Christian living (or, as Calvin would say, "sanctification"). Just soldiering is God-like simply because God does this sort of thing. That's why it is blasphemous to reprove just soldiering: That which is reproved—the use of force to restrain evil—is something God does Himself. To reprove the use of force in the restraint of evil is thus to reprove God.

God has given earthly government the power to maintain public order and peace, including the power to take up arms to execute public vengeance against enemies. Enemies from outside the kingdom, Calvin said, are like enemies from within—robbers and murderers. Just as the magistrate has a holy and lawful duty to pursue robbers and murderers, so the government has a holy and lawful duty to defend the commonwealth from outside enemies.

Calvin said nevertheless that rulers ought to seek peace by all means before resorting to war, and that wars should be waged not in anger or in order to vent passions on others, but only through necessity and with regard for the public good. And because soldiering is conceived as an office of love, Calvin rejected outright mercenary soldiering. Soldiers who fight merely for money do not fight out of love for their neighbors.[8]

WHY SHOULD CHRISTIANS FIGHT?

Let's now review some of the major points we've learned from Calvin, as well as tie up loose strands.

1. Why should Christians fight? The short answer is to say that Christians fight for justice because God is like that—He uses force to check evil and to bring justice. Christians ought to use force to restrain evil because God is like that; God's order demands it.

2. Because of human sin, God uses force to work out His will for us. This use of force is a product of His love. God even loves those whom He kills, whether by His own hand or by the hand of others.

3. Human political order is the structure God has given to encourage virtue and to restrain vice. In our fallen state, human beings have a difficult time becoming good without the use of force, and only through the

use of force can the state ensure justice and the making of a peaceful space for human beings to become truly human.

4. Just war is something Christians do in this world out of loving obedience to God and in conformity with His ways. Meanwhile, acts of force prompted by disordered passion (a passion not governed by love of God) are *not* God-like acts of force and are morally suspect for the Christian. The duty of the soldier can never be one of personal vengeance—a warning emphasized by Christ (Matthew 5:38-41).

Of course, Christians realize that ultimate and final justice is something that will have to wait until the end of history. But until God brings an end to history, He has chosen to work through the earthly governing authorities, as clumsy as this may be, in order to bring at least a modicum of justice for human beings.

We should not sneer at this imperfect justice, this "peace of Babylon," for it allows us to do things like go to church, buy groceries to feed our families, get an education, go to a ball game, take trips across the country or overseas to see relatives and friends, and participate in countless other activities that make this life less of a burden than it might be without them. Many of these things would be impossible if lawlessness ruled the land, and lawlessness would reign if it were not for governing authorities and the threatened use of force. As a medieval rabbi once remarked, a man would eat his neighbor alive if it were not for the state.

DOUBLE DEMAND

The Christian just warrior is someone who soldiers out of love for God and neighbor. Calvin conceived the duty of the soldier as a duty of love, and he viewed respect for the power of magistrates and their impartial wielding of that power as part of the law of love. From this perspective, we can see that John the Baptist's advice to soldiers is likewise a call to soldiering with love of neighbor as the one purpose.

The Old Testament gives us models of this kind of excellence in soldiering, men such as Joshua and David, whom Calvin saw as men of gentleness and meekness who were moved to great violence (*Institutes* IV.20.10).

Such soldiers are not simply born but made, and it takes a great deal of effort—and no little help from God—to be such a soldier. Nor is it any small work to shape the sort of people who can recognize when war is just and thus worthy of Christian support and participation.

The just war as a Christian endeavor rose to prominence in the early Middle Ages, so it isn't surprising to find fictional models of just warriors populating the literature of that period in history. In Malory's *The Death of Arthur*, the knight Lancelot is described as "the meekest man and the gentlest that ever ate in the hall among ladies" and also as "the sternest knight...that ever put spear in the rest" (XXI.13). Lancelot, so conceived, is the chivalric ideal of a Christian knight; he is the ideal Christian warrior.

History tells us, however, that the heroism demanded in combat is not something always achieved by the virtuous. In fact, there are times when it seems that it's the vicious who are needed to "get the job done."

Such an ideal, as C. S. Lewis once observed, puts a "double demand" on human nature.[9] For Lancelot represents not an ideal mean between meekness and violent prowess, but the highest degree of both at the same time.[10]

Yet, as C. S. Lewis rightly cautioned, "The knightly character is art not nature—something that needs to be achieved, not something that can be relied upon to happen."[11] How can the art of virtuous warfare be achieved, and what will it look like once it is attained? How does the Church go about shaping warriors in this mold, people who can wisely recognize when force is called for, and who then use force in ways consistent with holy Christian living?

To these questions we now turn.

CHAPTER THREE

Christian Virtue and Warfare

The Formation of Just War Leaders and Soldiers

The Christian just war tradition enables believers not only to judge *when* it's proper to support and encourage a war but also to be able to fight well in battle, in a way appropriate to followers of Jesus Christ. The just war doctrine is meant to restrain and control the use of violence in a just cause, but it also concerns the formation of leaders and soldiers who have to obey the doctrine.

Battle is to the strong, both morally and physically—which is to say that battle is to those with the greater will to endure violence and to give violence. Should the Church be in the business of shaping such people? And if so, how?

Traditional Christianity has declared that indeed the Church ought to be in the business of shaping such people, and it has done so through Christian nurture and discipline grounded in the moral language of Christian virtue, which itself has roots in Jewish, Greek, and Roman thought.

HITTING THE BULL'S-EYE

The importance of character is enormous for military ethics and the just war. Who will be able to formulate good laws of war if not the wise? Who will be able to follow those laws if not the courageous and self-controlled?

The problem of appropriate virtue in warfare, which has been a common one for moralists since Aristotle, is especially acute in the modern war context. In ancient and medieval times, mechanized and impersonal means of destruction and killing were thought to debilitate virtue. But such means have been the most common way of fighting since the beginning of the twentieth century. Nevertheless, nobility and virtue still are possible in modern warfare. When the cause is just, it is virtuous to fight well in battle, whether the soldier can accurately throw a spear or a grenade, shoot an arrow or a bullet straight, or skillfully ride a horse or pilot a fighter plane.

Technology does not remove the possibility of virtue, but it does increase the possibilities for vice. This is only to be expected, for in warfare, as in all other human activities, there's a very small area of potentially appropriate acts—only one small bull's-eye area in the moral target. But the possibilities for wrong acts—for missing the bull's-eye—are limitless. Every technological advance gives us one more small space for possible virtuous acts, but endless possibilities for vice.

We need leaders and soldiers who are prudent, courageous, self-controlled, and just. We need leaders and soldiers marked by the virtues that will empower them to know when to go to battle, what kind of battles to fight, and when to stop the fighting. We need leaders and soldiers who possess character that enables them to seek every opportunity for victory against the enemy, but who also are resolved to accept death before dishonor, for there can be no "just" war that is at the same time a "dishonorable" war.

AQUINAS AND VIRTUE

As we explore this topic further, let's look a bit closer at what Thomas Aquinas has contributed to our discussion of Christian just war doctrine.

Aquinas's moral approach to war is virtue driven. He was concerned, of course, with the virtue of justice, but what surprises the modern reader—even the modern Christian reader—is the prominence Aquinas gave to the virtue of love (charity) in discussing the violence of war.

The love of God, Aquinas said, is necessary for acquiring all other virtues (for we cannot even desire what is good without at the same time desiring God); in order to acquire excellence in any worthy practice, love is essential. Love and war are not incompatible, and war making must be a work of love if it is to be morally acceptable to the Christian. This means that a soldier cannot be an excellent Christian soldier without charity.

OUR HIGHER PURPOSE

To better grasp how Aquinas can help us understand and apply the Christian doctrine of just war, we want to look carefully in this chapter at several aspects of virtue.

Fundamentally, Aquinas argued that human beings were made by God with certain inborn inclinations such as self-preservation; the birth, nurture, and education of children; the pursuit of goods; and, most important of all, the pursuit of the knowledge of God. To be properly fulfilled, Aquinas said, these inclinations must be ordered and understood within the context of our larger purpose.

The logic of this position is clear. Think of a football team. The team can function well only when it's clearly understood why the team was created: to win football games, which is the whole point of forming a team and of pursuing the inclinations of running, blocking, throwing and kicking the ball, and so forth.

The same goes for human beings; when we know what we were created for, we can effectively pursue our inborn inclinations. Aquinas called this the "knowledge of the end." The "end" of something is the purpose for which it was created. The "end" of a pen is to write, the "end" of a chair is to be sat upon, and the "end" of a knife is to cut. Human beings seem to have a lot of ends (as reflected in all those natural, God-given inclinations previously mentioned), but only one final end, one larger governing purpose, which Aquinas called *beatitude*. Beatitude is that perfect state of happiness found in blessed communion with God, and ultimately in our place with God in the afterlife.

VIRTUES ENABLE FULFILLMENT OF PURPOSE

Virtues, meanwhile, are those dispositional character traits that enable us to act rightly in accordance with this purpose for which we were made.

A virtue is the character quality or the power that enables something to function as it is designed to function. The etymology of the English word *virtue* can help us understand more clearly what this means. The word *virtue* is used to translate the ancient Greek word *aretē,* which means "excellence," that is, excellent in terms of its function. Because the very purpose of a knife is to cut, an excellent knife is one that cuts well.

The Latin translation of *aretē* is *virtus,* a word that can also mean "power" or "ability." Here we're getting closer to the full meaning of the word *virtue.* A virtue is that which gives something the power or ability to function well as it ought. Just as we say that a knife is excellent (virtuous) in proportion to how well it cuts, so we say that human beings are excellent (virtuous) in proportion to how well they fulfill their function as human beings.

And what is the function of a human being? For what purpose did Aquinas say that human beings were made? Again, that purpose is to be in blessed communion with God—beatitude. Thus, human beings fulfill their function insofar as they act according to their end, which is beatitude with God. Broadly speaking, virtues are those character traits that give us the power to do this.

TWO KINDS OF VIRTUES

Aquinas spoke of two sorts of moral virtues—*acquired* and *infused.*

Acquired virtues can be learned and exercised by anyone, Christian or not. (These virtues are part of what Calvin called a "preserving grace" given by God in order to make human life tolerable; for example, God dispenses a certain amount of virtue to pagans in order for political regimes to run smoothly enough to make life possible.) Human beings have natural capacities for these virtues, which are conducive to a good civil society.

The *infused* moral virtues are those that Christians receive by God's grace. When we live by them, what we do is done for Christ's sake and ultimately by Christ's power. Christians receive from God infused moral virtues, including the virtues of faith, hope, and love, in order that we might have habits that enable us to act in accordance with our final end—beatitude.

We can know what actions are conformable to virtue by divine revelation—most notably through the Ten Commandments, which, Aquinas said, are the primary precepts of justice and law. Divine revelation, in fact, is the foundation for all knowledge about virtue, for divine revelation sets the standards for right action.

WE NEED TRAINING IN VIRTUE

Human beings may have a natural aptitude for virtue, but it needs to be trained. This is done in a number of ways.

Most important, we need the help of others. Just as an inexperienced car mechanic needs to learn his craft from an experienced one, so also those inexperienced in acting virtuously need help from those who are experienced. In his discussion of human law, Aquinas argued that it is

> difficult to see how man could suffice for himself
> in the matter of this training: since the perfection
> of virtue consists chiefly in withdrawing a man
> from undue pleasures, to which above all man is
> inclined, and especially the young, who are more
> capable of being trained. Consequently a man
> needs to receive this training from another,
> whereby to arrive at the perfection of virtue.
> (*Summa Theologica* I-II.95.1)

It's hard to learn virtue on your own. One of the main stumbling blocks is that human beings always like to take the easy way out when it comes to any task, but especially when it comes to tasks we don't want to do. Because our "old man" (to use Paul's phrase) is ever with us, we often do not want to do the good. We're addicted to "undue pleasures" that our old man revels in above all else. We need someone to help us. Most of all, we need the grace of God even to *want* to do what is good, but when it comes to the "hands-on" learning experience, a pupil achieves excellence in a practice only by learning from a master (someone who has already acquired excellence in that practice). This is how you learn to be a carpenter or a football player. It's also how you learn to be courageous, just, self-controlled, and wise. Timothy learned virtue from Paul, and we also learn it from those experienced in the godly life.

WHAT MORALITY IS

For Aquinas, any human act can be called either praiseworthy or blameworthy. Everything we do has moral content.

We aren't used to thinking about morality in this way. We're used to thinking about morality in some terrible dilemma—who should we save when five people are stranded in the desert with only enough food for four?—or in a moment of temptation, as when we see a man's wallet fall out of his coat pocket and must decide whether to give it back to him. When we have to make "momentous" decisions that affect people's lives in some immediately serious way, that's when we think we're handling a moral issue; when we're obviously good in the face of a tempting evil, that's when we think we're moral. And so we are.

But morality is about so much more than these things. Morality is about shaping our controlling attitudes and everyday behavior into the kind of character that is pleasing to God. Just about every human act is an act for or against God. Consequently, all human acts contribute to the virtuous or vicious character-information of each human being.

Human beings always act for a reason, and the reason tells us what sort of effect each action will have on their character. If our intentions are good, we're off to a right start. But a truly virtuous act also must be done at the right time and at the right place (the appropriate circumstances), as well as for the purpose of achieving some good end (right intention). Meanwhile, some acts can never be good; there's no such thing as "good" adultery, for adultery is inherently evil. Moral virtue is the reliable disposition toward acting well, time and again.

THE CARDINAL VIRTUES AND LOVE

Let's now look with Aquinas at the four so-called *cardinal virtues*, as well as at their relationship to love.

Prudence or wisdom is the exercise of reason; it enables us to know what we ought to do, when we ought to do it, and how. This virtue enables soldiers to make sound decisions in planning and fighting.

Justice is the virtue that grants a person the constant desire to render each person his due. A just person always seeks to give what is rightly owed to others. This is the virtue that, among other things, enables us to distinguish just wars from unjust wars. For Aquinas and Calvin, the precepts of the Ten Commandments, and those derived directly from them, were the basis for all justice.

Courage or fortitude is the control of those passions that drive us to act unreasonably or fearfully in the face of danger or hardship. The value of this virtue to the warrior is obvious, for soldiers regularly face life-threatening situations.

Temperance or self-control is the restraint of passions that are contrary to reason; it's the virtue that can check actions born from hate and revenge. Needless to say, temperance plays a crucial role in proper combat behavior.

We must keep in mind that love—not justice—is the crucial virtue in Christian soldiering. Justice is, of course, the key cardinal virtue insofar as we want to know what a "just" war looks like, but the virtue of love is what will give the impetus for Christian participation in a just war.

No one can be completely just without the virtue of love. Love is the "more excellent way" and "the greatest of these," Paul said in 1 Corinthians 13, and the Christian tradition beginning with Ambrose has held that love is the form of all virtue; it is the friendship of a human being for God, and no true virtue is possible without it. As a gift of grace from God, love guides the virtues in the right direction; love is always aiming at the good.

HOW VIRTUOUS ARE PAGAN VIRTUES?

A comparison with Augustine's account of human nature and virtue in *The City of God* is helpful in drawing the contours of Aquinas's perspective more clearly. In Augustine's view, the earthly citizen is marked by, among other things, the inability to attain any true virtue, and the story of the two cities tells us why this is so. In *The City of God*, Augustine said that the earthly city began with the fallen angels who possessed evil wills and delighted in themselves instead of God. Human beings fell for the same reason—love of self over love of God. By exercising the preference of self over God, human beings have slipped into a bestial condition where the original misuse of free will has started a chain of disasters from which only God can save us.

Those driven by evil wills desire to live by their own standards instead of God's standard, which is the standard of truth. This love of self is what citizens of the earthly kingdom share and what marks them most. According to Augustine, such people cannot possibly attain true virtue. Pagan virtue is virtue only insofar as it is modeled on true virtue, which must be informed by perfect love.

Aquinas affirmed much of the Augustinian account: Pagan virtues are not guided by love; pagan virtues therefore cannot lead the virtuous to their ultimate end. Pagan virtues are deficient because they lack the necessary and correct goal. Aquinas also agreed with Augustine that charity is the form of all virtue and that acquired moral virtues not guided by charity are deficient.

Yet, for Aquinas, who had read deeply in Aristotle, earthly limited good *can* be attained by means of acquired moral virtue without love. In Aquinas's view—and here he departed from Augustine—this does not mean that pagan virtues are counterfeit virtues; they are real virtues, but without love to inform them, they are deficient and cannot lead the person to God.

On this point, Calvin was closer to Aquinas than to Augustine. Calvin agreed with Aquinas that pagan virtues are real virtues because God gives them to certain human beings in order to preserve the political order. Nevertheless, for Augustine as well as for Aquinas and Calvin, a right relationship to God is needed for the virtues to be all they can be—for the virtues to be oriented toward our final end of blessed communion with God.

THE ORDER OF LOVE

There existed for Aquinas an order of love: We owe certain people more love than we do others, and we owe God the most love of all. This is not to deny that Christians ought to love everyone equally, but the "equally" here means that "all men ought to be loved equally insofar as we ought to wish for all of them the same good, viz., eternal life" (*On Charity* Q.8, reply to obj. 8).

First in the order of love is love of God before all. Next, the common good is sought above even my own good, since love for myself makes no sense apart from the common good. Love also discriminates between neighbors in that we love nearby neighbors in more ways than distant neighbors. Finally, love for blood kin is stronger than love for neighbors.

When it comes to preferences in how we act toward others, the subject matter tells us what to do: In matters of state, we should prefer our fellow citizens; in matters on the battlefield, we should prefer our fellow soldiers. This is why, for example, Aquinas argued that we ought to show "more of the effects of love" toward our parents than toward nonfamily members,

> except if by chance, when the common good
> which each one ought also desire for himself
> would depend on the good of someone who is
> not a member of one's family, as when one would
> expose himself to the danger of death in order to
> save the general of the army in war time, or to save

the leader of a state insofar as the welfare of the
entire community depends on these men. (*On
Charity* Q.8, reply to obj. 15)

There was, then, no inherent conflict for Aquinas between love
and acts of force. The order of love admits preferences for loved
ones, fellow citizens, and fellow soldiers, and all these preferences
sometimes call for acts of force.

KNOWING GOD THROUGH THE MORAL LAW

Let's now turn again to Calvin to explore the role played by the
moral law in learning virtue.

The Old Testament moral law still plays a necessary role in the
Christian's life. Human salvation is no longer dependent upon our
keeping the moral law on our own, but human beings still must
keep the moral law because this is how we please God and fulfill
our purpose as human beings.

The purpose of the moral law is to guide Christian behavior,
for it is a reflection of God's righteousness. When we read about
God's moral law in Scripture, we learn that we cannot possibly follow the law without the virtues that God grants to us through His
grace by the Holy Spirit.

When Calvin discussed the summation of the moral law—the
Ten Commandments—he argued that the vices forbidden by the
Ten Commandments imply the virtues we need in order to obey
God's will. Thus, the Ten Commandments command virtue while

they condemn vice. The commandment, "You shall not kill" (Exodus 20:13) does not merely mean that we should abstain from killing but also requires us to help the life of our neighbor all that we can. God forbids us to take a life unjustly, but, at the same time, He requires us to do all we can to preserve life. The very purpose of the commandment not to kill is to show us that the Lord has bound humankind together in such a way that each person ought to be concerned with the safety of everyone else. The command not to kill means that we ought to seek peace if we can and avoid harming others (in accordance with Paul's advice in his letter to the Romans), but if anyone is in danger, we ought to help, even if it means using force.

The reason why God gave the command not to kill is that human beings are made in His image. To do harm to a human being is thus to violate the image of God. But we should keep in mind that we also violate this command when we fail to help someone who is in danger that we could have helped. When we fail to use force to protect others, we do harm to the image of God. We also fail to take an additional step on the road to our being made more fit for beatitude with Him. We fail to act like God when we refuse to use force in a just cause.

THE VIRTUES, GRACE, AND GOOD WORKS

Calvin left ample room for the moral virtues in his discussion of the benefits and effects of grace, but the virtues we have are from God. Furthermore, order in the world demands that we distinguish between the vices and virtues of unbelievers. This distinction is from the Lord Himself, and, in fact, God bestows blessings even on the unbelievers who practice virtue. Yet this does not mean that unbelievers (or believers) merit redemption because of virtue. Rather it means that God graciously bestows temporal benefit on the virtuous unbeliever for the benefit of the political order.

Calvin and Aquinas agreed that the Christian moral life is a growing process in which the moral virtues, as gifts from God, serve as the tools that shape the believer's character such that the believer becomes more fit for the final end of human beings: blessedness with God. The role of the moral law in all this is to provide a guide for virtuous behavior. God's commands indicate to us what kinds of behavior are in accord with His sanctifying grace.

Calvin emphasized that Jesus Christ accomplishes both our justification and our sanctification together. To separate the two would mean, for Calvin, to separate the Christian moral life from that which makes such a life possible.

The Christian moral life is, nevertheless, a life of doing good works. How can Christians do good works? For Calvin, sanctification is nothing less than having your character formed in a way consonant with God's purposes for our beatitude with Him. Calvin argued that we must have a heart transformed so that it can love God and act accordingly with a right motive. For Calvin, perfection in the moral life is single-minded devotion to God's will and sincere behavior in accordance with that devotion.[1] Such single-minded devotion and sincere behavior indicate a complete change of character. Our good works proceed from a character that has been redirected to obey the will of God.

COMPELLED BY THE HOLY SPIRIT

A first glance at Calvin can be misleading, for he often talked as if the Christian life can be characterized as "mechanical" rule following. For example, he argued that God "has so depicted His character in the law that if any man carries out in deeds whatever is enjoined there, he will express the image of God, as it were, in his own life" (*Institutes* II.8.51).

Calvin added, however, that the moral law helps us know what counts as true virtue. The moral law is, for the believer, no longer an instrument of death, a reminder of sin; instead, "through the activity of the Holy Spirit," the law becomes an "active principle" of the believer's sanctification.[2] The moral life, therefore, is not a life of "mechanical" rule following, but a life of obeying God's will, and God's will can be obeyed only insofar as the believer is equipped with the virtues to do so.

Christians follow the moral law because it pleases God. God is pleased when we follow the moral law, for by doing so we're made more fitting for union with Him; that is, we're made more like Him. The moral precepts of the Old Law are an obliging force to Christians, but not a compelling force, for what compels Christians to act well is the Holy Spirit, a gift to us through the Father's love. Love, therefore, inclines the Christian to do what the moral law requires. Love inclines believers to do that which brings them closer to God. The Holy Spirit equips us for union with God by indwelling us and turning us into creatures more like God. The Holy Spirit begins the job of instilling in human beings divine characteristics here on earth in preparation for our ultimate end as human beings, and one way the Holy Spirit does this is to impel us to follow the moral law.

RIGHTEOUSNESS AND GROWTH

According to Calvin, the moral law is the "true and eternal rule of righteousness" (*Institutes* IV.20.15). The purpose of the moral law is to guide Christian behavior, for it is a reflection of God's righteousness. We learn from the law that God is our Father, that He is merciful and holy, and that He requires obedience. We also learn that we need the virtues to follow the moral law. In his explanation of the moral law (*Institutes* II.8), Calvin argued that virtue is not simply the opposite of vice; the condemnation of a vice implies the commandment of a virtue. So the moral law commands virtue as well as forbids vice.

Following Augustine and Aquinas, Calvin argued that the virtues of unbelievers are best thought of as images of virtue, for there is no true virtue without faith. The believers who practice virtue do so out of zeal for the good (a zeal given to believers by the grace of God), but unbelievers practice virtue out of ambition, self-love, or some other corrupted motive. (Augustine and Aquinas would say "a disordered passion.") We must remember that a good act, if it is to be fully good, is one done to serve God. So all acts done for other motives cannot be fully good acts, strictly speaking. When the end of our act of force is a zeal for a true good—that is, for God—it is an act worthy of reward. We consider such acts worthy of reward because they are God-like acts, powered by the Holy Spirit, which makes us more fit for our ultimate end with God.

Consequently, in Calvin's view there is real moral growth in sanctification. From God's perspective, of course, nothing is lacking in our salvation; we're justified and sanctified by the work of Jesus Christ. But we cannot see things from God's perspective. From our perspective, we don't see the evidence of an immediate and complete change of character. Thus our sanctification, from our point of view, is a work in progress, to be completed in the life to come.

WAR AS A POSITIVE GOOD

Finally—with the background of Aquinas's thoughts on virtue and Calvin's teaching on the moral law and Christian living—let's conclude by showing how the approach to warfare exemplified by Aquinas and Calvin looks at war not as a "necessary evil" but as a positive good for Christians.

Virtue and the common good are the pivots of the classical Christian account of the just war. When Aquinas considered the vices opposed to love (hatred, sloth, envy, discord, contention, schism, strife, sedition, scandal), war is not one of them (*ST* II-II.34-43). Later, he said that war is contrary to peace, but that is not always a bad thing, since peace is not always a just order worth preserving. War is a means to a just peace and a means to break an unjust peace (such as one imposed by, say, the Nazis). Peace, therefore, is not a virtue in itself but only the purpose of just war. We keep the peace and fight just wars because these are acts of love and, hence, meritorious acts.

Modern Christian pacifists have argued that a presumption against violence is what led Christians to create just war criteria in the first place. But this claim is historically false. Christians did not create the just war criteria out of a disregard for violence but because they wished to bring some sort of justice and order to this temporal existence. Aquinas and Calvin certainly knew of no such presumption against violence.

When Aquinas discussed the New Law and its relationship to the Old Law, he said that "the intention of the [Old] Law was that retaliation should be sought out of love of justice...and this remains still in the New Law" (*ST* I-II.107.2, cf. 108.3). In his commentary on Paul's letter to the Romans, where he discussed the role of the governing authorities (13:1-7), Aquinas said that it is not only allowable but positively "meritorious for Princes to exercise vindication of justice with zeal against bad people" (*Commentary on Romans* 13, lect. i). Moreover, in the discussion of murder (*ST* II-II.64), he insisted that it is both "praiseworthy and advantageous" for someone with the proper authority to kill someone dangerous and infectious to the community (64.2). This accords with Aquinas's argument that vindication is a virtue when it is sought for the good of the community (*ST* II-II.108). Thus, while peace is not a virtue, proper vindication is.

When we add these comments by Aquinas to what has been shown previously, we have strong reasons to suggest that, for

Aquinas, the presumption is not against violence but against injustice. In his view, love does not merely allow for violent action, it actually demands it.

WHY JUSTIFY WAR?

What, then, is the point of the just war doctrine? If there is no presumption against violence and war, why does war need to be justified?

War needs to be justified because going to war will lead inevitably to all kinds of suffering. Also, because fallen human beings can never be certain of their intentions, especially in desperate situations, we can never be sure that we will not commit unjust acts in war. Indeed, just warriors recognize that they will do unjust things in war because they are not perfect, and they realize that they can act well in combat only to the extent that they have acquired the virtues that will enable them to do so in extreme conditions. Thus, those who decide upon war must ensure that they have sifted out as much as possible any evil desires that may lie behind their decision for war. Warfare is not something to be entered into lightly and must, as time permits, be considered carefully. This is why the virtues should be in place before a crisis appears.

War entails great suffering, but we don't decide against war because of that suffering; rather, we say that we must make sure of the justice of our cause before we proceed. We do this to prevent the intended evil that would occur should we enter a war for unjust reasons.

Of course, just war defenders may often speak disapprovingly of war, but this is not because they consider the use of force to be somehow evil in itself or out of step with holy Christian living and therefore in need of justification. Their "presumption" against war is roughly like a physician's presumption against surgery. The ability to perform surgery, especially high-risk, complicated surgery, is a distinguishing mark of the excellent physician. Nevertheless, because surgery can be risky and lead to unforeseen and unintended complications, surgeons ought not to rush to perform surgery unless they're skilled enough both in diagnosis and surgery to know when and how the procedure should be done. We don't call such surgical procedures evil procedures that need justifying. Instead we say that such procedures carry enough grave risks that we ought to be careful about when we perform them.[3]

AQUINAS AND THE CLERGY

A final point from Aquinas for this chapter: Aquinas maintained the traditional prohibition against bishops and clergy fighting in war, for two reasons. He said participation in war keeps them from their proper duties, and that shedding blood is "unbecoming" for those who serve the body and blood of Christ to Christians in the Eucharist (*ST* II-II.40.2).

There's no doubt that Aquinas considered the duties of bishops and clerics more meritorious than those of soldiers, but this does not mean that the soldier's duties have no merit. Aquinas employed an analogy with marriage to make his point clear: It is meritorious to marry but better still to remain a virgin and thus dedicate yourself wholly to spiritual concerns; likewise, it is meritorious to fight just wars and restrain evil, but more meritorious still to be a bishop and give the Eucharist.

Nevertheless, bishops and clergy ought to urge and counsel others to engage in just wars and to offer spiritual help to the military, which is more meritorious than actual physical participation in warfare. Aquinas also approved of prayers that ask God to inflict temporal ills on enemies. Aquinas clearly did not seek to keep the bishops and clergy free of military concerns.

LOOKING AGAIN AT CHRIST'S MEEKNESS

And a final point from Calvin: We saw earlier how Calvin looked upon just soldiering as a holy vocation and held that to reprove this vocation is to blaspheme God. Calvin declared that to soldier justly— to restrain evil out of love for neighbor—is a God-like act, the sort of thing God Himself does. He restrains evil out of love for His creatures. Just war acts are God-like insofar as they restrain evil and are done out of love for the neighbor—both the neighbor we protect and the unjust neighbor who is the object of our acts of violence.

None of this is to say that we *fully* imitate God or Christ when we use force justly, for the just warrior's acts can never be redemptive acts—acts that have a saving quality for those who are the targets of our force (except in the sense that the just warrior "saves" the unjust neighbor from committing further unjust acts). This sort of love cannot save the unjust aggressor—it cannot overcome the distance between that person and God. In this sense at least, the just warrior may be said to be one who, as the Reformers liked to say, follows Christ at a distance.

For Calvin, Christ's pacific nature carries little normative weight for Christians, for that pacific nature is located in Christ's priestly office of reconciliation and intercession—an office that Christians can in no way fulfill or reproduce. Christ's pacific nature—His willingness to suffer death at the hands of unjust authorities both Jewish and Roman—is inextricably tied to His role as Redeemer and is not meant to be a complete model for Christian behavior. No Christian can follow Christ as a Redeemer, but all can follow Christ as One who obeys the commands of the Father.

CHAPTER FOUR

When Christians Should Fight

The Criteria of Jus ad Bellum

With help from the early Church Fathers and from Aquinas and Calvin, we've concluded that Christians have good reason for using force: It can bring a just peace.

But not every use of force brings a just peace, or is even intended to do so. Because warfare entails such great suffering, Christians must be wary of using force. How can we tell if a war is just? How can we know when the time and circumstances are right for resorting to force?

The Christian just war tradition has formulated a number of criteria to help Christians make such decisions. These rules of war are commonly known by their Latin name, *jus ad bellum,* which means simply "justice toward war." The goal in using these criteria is to figure out where justice lies in a proposed conflict. Should we fail to justify the war, we have to say no to entering the conflict.

The Christian tradition has typically settled on five criteria for *jus ad bellum:* (1) proper authority, (2) just cause, (3) right intention, (4) war as the only way to right the wrong, and (5) reasonable hope of success. Each criterion has both a positive and a negative connotation. Like the Ten Commandments, each rule both commands and forbids.

In general, we may say that when *all five criteria* are met, Christians have a duty to fight the war; and when *any one* of these criteria cannot be met, Christians are forbidden to fight.

1. PROPER AUTHORITY

For a war to be just, it must be declared and waged by someone who truly has the authority to do so. No matter how large a following you may have behind you, if you aren't the sovereign leader of the land, you cannot declare a war—at least not a just war.

A nation's sovereign leaders are entrusted with the care of that nation; thus they're responsible for the well-being of the population they govern. We who live in a representative democracy elect people to govern us. We expect them to do many things, but the very least we expect of them is protection from any neighbors both near and distant who would unjustly harm us. The government provides a police force for the former and a military for the latter.

Many who lived in ancient and medieval times had a particular horror of the anarchy brought by civil war—war waged from within a nation against its sovereign leaders. These wars usually led to the most brutal forms of fighting and long periods of lawlessness throughout the land. Luther had in mind this horror of civil war when he warned that anyone who makes war on a lawful prince, regardless of how worthless the prince might be, was guilty of participating in an unjust war.[1]

Calvin was the first major figure in the Christian tradition to argue that Christians could participate in a rebellion if the lawful authority was corrupt. In Calvin's eyes, a corrupt sovereign power was not actually "lawful," and, therefore, force could be justly used against it. Nevertheless, even Calvin affirmed that not just anyone could lead such a lawful rebellion, but only someone in a place of authority.

2. JUST CAUSE

Those whom we attack must deserve to be attacked on account of some wrong that they have done.

Augustine listed a number of specific just causes, including self-defense against an aggressor, restoring what has been unjustly seized, avenging wrongs, and punishing an unjust nation. Few people would argue with those first two—defending citizens from attack or restoring what was wrongly seized from citizens. What worries many modern minds is the obligation to avenge wrongs and to punish unjust nations. What's the point of revenge? Do we have a right to punish other nations?

There's no point to revenge if all it means is satisfying some burning desire to see others suffer as we have suffered. This "eye for an eye" justice has passed away for Christians, and they can play no part in it. But there's more to avenging wrongs than taking an eye for an eye. When our government avenges wrongs done to citizens, it shows everyone—especially potential offenders—that it does not take such offences lightly. Of course, military strikes may not be the best way to go about this; the virtue of prudence is that it helps us decide the best way.

In a certain respect, no single nation has a right to punish another nation for wrongs committed. In our world today, the United Nations technically reserves for itself the right to redress wrongs among nation-states, a position that member states of the UN acknowledge. (The willingness of these nations to submit to UN sovereignty in international disagreements is the direct result of their fear of a large-scale modern war. Also, we've seen in recent history that even the United States, an unrivaled superpower, has been unwilling to fully "go it alone" in international conflicts, but to some degree at least works through the UN and the international community.) This does not mean that punishing a nation is now an unjust form of warfare; it simply means that the United States and other nations have theoretically agreed to allow the UN the privilege of being the only entity with the proper authority to sanction such a war.

Christians must say no to proposed wars in which the people being attacked do not deserve to be attacked. The Christian cannot hold fast the motto "My country, right or wrong." Instead, the Christian must say, "I may not want to disown my country for some unjust act, but I will not attack another country unjustly if my country is in the wrong."

Christians cannot support injustice even when it appears we are being unpatriotic. As Augustine taught us, our earthly city is not the City of God. Christians are primarily citizens of God's kingdom, and this will always take precedence over any earthly citizenship. As the apostles said, "We must obey God rather than men" (Acts 5:29). When our nation declares an unjust war, we must obey God rather than our nation.

3. RIGHT INTENTION

Right intention means that we must intend our use of force to advance the good and to avoid the evil. When our aims are to secure peace, to punish those who perpetrate evil on the innocent, or to uplift the good, we exhibit right intention.

Right intention also means a war must have clear aims. The lack of clearly stated goals is more often than not an indication of indefensible motives such as revenge or the pursuit of ill-gotten gains through plundering a defeated nation.

4. WAR AS THE ONLY WAY TO RIGHT THE WRONG

Because warfare brings such human suffering, we should try to right wrongs by means other than warfare if we can, just as good doctors resort to surgery only when it's the sole way to heal the patient.

Our government has an obligation to see that justice is done in the most efficient and least burdensome manner possible. As the old saying goes, you don't use a baseball bat to kill a fly that has landed on another person's head. You don't go to war to right *every* wrong. Even ancient Sparta was not that warlike.

Many recent ethicists have championed a criterion called "last resort," in recognition of our impatient nature to take an eye for an eye when some injustice is done to us. Unfortunately, this approach has been so badly misused in the past few decades that it has become a worthless criterion. It appears to exist only to give those people who are dead set against any proposed conflict a ground for resisting any actual fighting. There's no real possibility of meeting the criterion of last resort if we take it literally, for there's always *something* we can do rather than go to war—even to the point of complete capitulation to an invading army.

But couldn't the same reasoning apply to the criterion of war as the only possible means to right a wrong? How could we ever know when war is the *only* possible means to do so? Can't the same people who always cry "last resort" switch their tactics and exclaim, "We can always seek justice in some other way"?

Well, yes and no. There will always be those who can abuse any just war criterion for their own ends. But when we say a proposed war is the *only* possible means to right a wrong, it's possible to have objective reasons for such a claim. For example, objective analysis would quite reasonably conclude that by the time World War II erupted, there simply was no way to overcome the evils of Hitler and Nazi Germany other than waging war against them. But at least as far as the United States was concerned, declaring war on Germany was definitely not the Americans' "last resort" in 1941, although this was more clearly the case for Britain when the *Luftwaffe* began bombing British cities a year earlier.

5. REASONABLE HOPE OF SUCCESS

There's simply no point in sacrificing so many lives and causing so much suffering in war if we have no chance of succeeding in the fight. Of course, we have to ask exactly what we mean by "success" in war. Many would argue that such success is not synonymous with "winning." Let's take two examples.

When Britain seemed to be on the brink of defeat in the early days of World War II, Prime Minister Winston Churchill gave a stirring speech in which he said the British would continue resisting regardless of how hopeless the cause—they would retreat into the hills and fight "until the last man dies choking in his own blood." Of course, we have to make allowances for rhetoric; after all, Churchill was trying to stiffen the backbone of a country that had suffered much and was about to suffer much more at the hands of the Nazis. But let's take the rhetoric seriously for a moment. Would it be just to sacrifice *everyone's* life in a hopeless cause? The alternative was surrender, and that meant being governed by Nazis. It's easy to say, "I would rather die than be governed by Nazis," but should even the leader of a nation make that decision for everyone, including future generations? Was Nazi rule really *that* bad?

I don't mean in any way to trivialize the evils perpetrated by the Nazis; all I'm asking is whether the extinction of a nation is worth the price of not being ruled by Nazis for a period of time—even a long period of time. Churchill spoke of a "new dark age" if Germany defeated Britain, but that dark age would eventually come to an end, as all ages do. Why not bide one's time for the sake of future generations?

Let's now make a different assumption. Suppose one nation decides to sacrifice itself for the good of another group of nations. Let's assume, for example, that Churchill's Britain was in a position to occupy the German military while its overseas allies—the United States, Canada, Australia, New Zealand, and others—gained time to build up their arms for sustaining the conflict in the future. Britain might not be able to save itself, but it could in the long run help cause Germany's defeat by fighting "to the last man." This would be a heroic act of charity on Britain's part, an act no other nation could possibly demand of that "tiny island," but one that Britain could will for itself if it so desired. "Success" here would be measured in how much time and effort the Nazis had to expend in bringing Britain to subjection. If the British kept their enemy occupied until the other Allies were ready to strike back, success would be achieved regardless of any other factors. Such a scenario is not simply suicidal, but one of love for other nations and for a way of life precious in the sight of those willing to sacrifice themselves in order to see it continue.

In summary, reasonable hope for success can be defined in ways other than the immediate surrender of enemy forces. Success may simply mean delaying or preventing the enemy from realizing unjust goals. However, suicidal acts meant only to spare us from experiencing a great evil are themselves evil and are not justifiable.

AN IMPROPER CRITERION: "COMPARATIVE JUSTICE"

Modern versions of the just war doctrine often include a criterion known as comparative justice. I've left it out of the previous list with good purpose: It's a bad criterion.

The comparative justice criterion asks us to weigh which side is "sufficiently right" in a proposed conflict. It assumes that *each* side is unjust, and we must figure out who is *more* unjust, and whether it's worth the trouble for the less unjust side to right a wrong through war, especially considering that it isn't very just in itself. Comparative justice assumes that we can never be sure who is really just or whose side God is really on. We can't know these things because no one is absolutely just.

However, admitting that we aren't perfect doesn't mean we cannot recognize when the imperfect actions of others need to be stopped. The Allies in World War II, for example, did not themselves have to be absolutely just to recognize that the Nazis were unjust and needed to be overcome.

Why do many modern ethicists embrace comparative justice? Perhaps it's because the virtues play no role for them in shaping warfare. To get the job done, they must invoke another rule: the suppression of pride and self-righteousness that may lead to vicious war making.

For Christians, however, cultivating the virtue of prudence helps us accurately determine when and how to combat injustice. Christians realize that they too "fall short of the glory of God" (Romans 3:23), but they can still recognize when others fall so short that they need restraining.

Nevertheless, those who promote the criterion of comparative justice have a legitimate worry. If history tells us anything, it's that nations usually like to get their citizens on the war-fighting bandwagon by inciting a crusading spirit. In such propaganda, the enemy is typically dehumanized to the point of beastliness, while our own cause is glorified to the point of pure righteousness. The criterion of comparative justice might then be valued because it helps short-circuit such pride and blind self-righteousness and the dehumanization of the enemy.

But comparative justice is not the best way to go about this, for it makes justice nearly impossible to achieve, and in effect takes the "justice" out of just war. It does this because it divorces justice from the other virtues. It says we cannot know where true justice lies, thereby divorcing justice from prudence, for in truth the just warrior's prudence is at one with his conscience. It emphasizes that we should hesitate to restrain evil, seeing that we are evil ourselves, and thereby divorces justice from courage. It divorces justice from temperance as it teaches us to do a lesser evil in order to prevent a greater one.

Love must guide justice and the other cardinal virtues—prudence, courage, and temperance—toward their proper end, with all working in harmony to bring the believer toward beatitude with

God. Fighting just wars is one way this is done, but comparative justice in essence denies that this could ever be possible, and it denies that the soldier can ever use force in such a way that the soldier is brought closer to God.

CHRISTIAN JUST WAR DOCTRINE AND THE MODERN LIBERAL STATE

Some will point out a potentially significant problem for the moral position we've sketched here of *jus ad bellum* as arising from the Christian just war tradition. Calvin and Aquinas wrote in a time when everyone assumed that the Church and the governing authorities work together for the common good. But this is certainly not the case today, especially in the United States, which insists on a Church and state so separated that the state cannot even give the appearance of privileging Christianity. In some eyes, the state has a positive duty to ignore all religious teaching and especially the teachings of Christianity. The state has to remain religiously neutral. So instead of providing for the common good by promoting good morals, the state should simply provide for a safe place where people from many traditions can exist together without cutting each other's throats. This sort of bare-bones protection still allows us to prosper, at least to some degree, in intermediary moral communities such as the Church.

But if bare-bones protection is all a citizen can expect from the state, one may wonder whether that state commands no more loyalty from its citizens than a protection racketeer does from its clients, as one observer has noted.[2] And any claim to the citizen's loyalty becomes even weaker if the effectiveness of the state's protection becomes as unstable and unpredictable as that offered by a racketeer.

When the state does little more than provide basic protection, and when it insists it has a positive duty to make sure it isn't influenced by Christianity, Christians might find it difficult to support such a government, particularly in wartime.

Alasdair MacIntyre has outlined a useful meeting ground, I believe, for Christians and the modern nation-state ethos on moral practices in war. He has identified four principles that complete and update the *jus ad bellum* for Christians living in today's liberal nation-state system:

1. The only justification for war is either self-defense (to preserve our liberty) or to preserve a people's liberty that we have pledged to uphold.

2. We must not use greater force than is necessary to preserve liberty.

3. We must not fail to threaten or wage war whenever we're confronted with the loss of liberty for ourselves or for those we've pledged to support.

4. We ought not to pledge military assistance to those whom we ought not or cannot defend.[3]

In MacIntyre's first principle, the thing we notice immediately is the narrower view of just cause. Traditionally, a just cause could be for more than self-defense or the protection of a neighbor state; it could also be for punishment of an offending state and the right to redress a wrong.

MacIntyre's second principle has pride of place in the just war criterion of right intention. Christians who adhere to the just war doctrine insist that a just war is a war with limited aims. The amount of force a just nation uses on its enemies is the amount of force it takes to reach the limited goals set at the beginning of the war. The failure to declare limited aims at the beginning of the war typically leads to overkill in the use of force. The lack of a limited objective soon translates into an unlimited goal such as the complete elimination of a nation's sovereignty with nothing to take its place and no way to care for the innocent civilians who survive the indiscriminate destruction. The amount of force needed for unlimited goals is usually unlimited. This leads to grave injustices that just war defenders cannot countenance. Using too much force betrays a lack of good intention.

In MacIntyre's third principle, the positive demand for engagement in war when justice is threatened fits nicely with the just war tradition's demand for engagement in those same instances. Should a nation fail to go to war to defend itself or another nation it has pledged to protect, that nation's government has failed, since a minimal requirement for good government is protection for the citizenry from outside threats. Likewise, the failure to help someone you've pledged to uphold is a breakdown in minimum decency. No nation can call itself just when it fails to live up to such agreements, especially when such agreements undergird the very life of another nation.

Of course this means we have to be careful with regard to making agreements to support other nations, and such caution is what

MacIntyre's fourth principle calls for. We ought not, for instance, pledge assistance to a nation led by a corrupt regime—of which there seem to be as many examples today as ever. Or, to take a concrete example from the past, if we had fully understood the facts, we might well have stayed out of the Vietnam conflict after concluding that South Vietnam wasn't the kind of ally we should be facilitating (nor was North Vietnam, for that matter).

This caution also requires that we determine how much force we're willing to expend engaging in conflict for "humanitarian purposes," and whether this would be enough to get the job done. To cite another twentieth-century example, clearly the American level of commitment did not match the level of need in Somalia in the early 1990s.

CONCLUSION

Warfare brings hardship and tests a nation's character as nothing else does; we simply cannot fight a war without causing suffering to those we do not wish to see suffer—innocent civilians and our own soldiers. Therefore, Christians should support their nation in war only when the war is just, and this is precisely where the just war doctrine aids us.

When Christians declare that the war proposed by their nation meets the five criteria set forth in the traditional Christian doctrine of just war, they should support their nation. Failure to do so would mean a failure to love and a failure to please God. But if the proposed war fails to meet any one of the five criteria, Christians should refuse to support the war, and we should protest it with all our strength.

Both support for a war and protest against a war demand much from the Church. Is the Church preparing its people to meet these demands? We can only pray that it is.

CHAPTER FIVE

How Christians Should Fight

The Criteria for Jus in Bello

To many modern ears, it sounds strange: For *love's* sake Christians fight in a just war, according to the traditional doctrine as conceived by Ambrose, Augustine, Aquinas, and Calvin.

But how can acts of force be loving?

We could give a short answer by pointing out an everyday example: A mother punishes her child, with force if necessary, because she loves him; likewise, out of love she will use violence, if necessary, to protect her child. Such a simple reply is too easy, but the point is a good one to start with: Acts of force can be loving acts.

As we saw before, God uses force on human beings because He loves us. Sometimes this force is gentle, sometimes not. God gave to human political order the responsibility of using force for His own appointed reasons—to protect and reward the good and to punish and restrain evil. When we use force for these God-ordained reasons, we're doing loving acts modeled on God's love for His creation.

But the Christian obligation to participate in just wars does not mean that once the war is begun, Christians have no limitations in how they wage it; their acts in war are limited for love's sake. We must pursue these loving acts of force in a loving way.

This second part of the Christian just war doctrine—the *how* of fighting a just war—is known as *jus in bello,* which means "justice in war," or we might say, "just means" in war fighting. *Jus in bello* provides rough guidelines for virtuous combat behavior, guidelines that put broad strictures around what can count as just war fighting.

NO CONSENT TO EVIL

As an overarching principle, pursuing any action for love's sake and in a God-pleasing way means that we can never do evil that good might come. We're never to do a "lesser evil" in order to avoid a greater one. Paul once told his Roman readers that we ought not to sin in order to receive more grace (Romans 6:1-2). This admonition had a great impact on Western Christianity. In *The City of God,* Augustine discussed the possibility of lawful suicide, and, in particular, whether Christians could kill themselves in order to avoid rape or torture and a long, painful death. Augustine denied that Christians can commit suicide for any reason and insists that "courage decides to endure evil rather than to consent to evil" (I.18). This should be the motto of Christian just war doctrine, indeed of all Christian ethics.

Fighting justly in a just cause is not an evil, but a good—an act of love—that is pleasing to God; fighting unjustly is an evil for which there is never an excuse. When we do things like killing innocent people deliberately, even if it is to spare more lives in the long run, we do evil that good might come, and this is wrong. For Paul, for Augustine, and indeed for the rest of the Christian tradition, it is better for Christians to lose their own lives than to do evil in order to preserve them.

Arising from this principle of never doing evil that good may come are the two guidelines of discrimination and proportion. *Discrimination* (or noncombatant immunity) says that we ought to target only those who deserve targeting; we discriminate between those who are proper military targets and those who are not. *Proportion* reminds us that the good results from our acts of force need to be worth the suffering they cause.

How these two criteria work together has been a great bone of contention among ethicists. Does the discrimination guideline mean that we've done something immoral every time an innocent person is killed in a military action? Since no war was ever fought in which no innocent person was killed, is *every* war unjust? Or does it mean perhaps that proportion decides the matter in the end—we estimate how many innocent lives we must jeopardize to get the job done, then determine whether getting the job done outweighs that likely cost?

DISCRIMINATION OR NONCOMBATANT IMMUNITY

The first and foremost guideline in *jus in bello* is that no innocent people are to be targeted intentionally.

This means that we should never plan to target innocent civilians directly, for we have seen in the previous chapter (under the *jus ad bellum* criterion of "right intention") that part of the very meaning of a just war is that we intend to attack only those who deserve to be attacked. When we combat the enemy, this principle constrains us both to never *intentionally* kill the innocent, and to do all we can to *avoid* killing the innocent.

Avoiding unintentional suffering for innocent people arises as an issue when we try to determine if our hoped-for success in our battle strategy is worth the suffering it will cause to the innocent as an unintentional by-product. The key here is the phrase "unintentional by-product." We must never *intend* to harm innocent people as a means to achieving victory. Killing the innocent can play no role in answering the question, "Why did you attack this target at this time and in this way?"

Noncombatant immunity is a guideline that Christians as well as others in our culture are particularly loath to transgress. Judaism and Islam also claim this principle in their traditional moral strictures on combat behavior. Likewise, throughout history various secular codes of war have regularly promoted such discrimination for a variety of reasons, but mainly for reasons of personal glory—after all, in most cultures a soldier wins little renown for killing women, children, the elderly, or the sick. Nevertheless, military necessity has traditionally overridden concern for the innocent in secular codes of war. Christian just war doctrine, on the contrary, will play no part in such thinking, and this standard is one of its most distinctive features.

The concern for love lies behind the Christian emphasis on noncombatant immunity. If the very reason Christians fight is for the sake of love, we should not do unloving things in war such as killing innocent people intentionally. Nevertheless, what counts as "innocence" in war is a matter determined by prudence and justice—not by love. Love cannot help us discriminate in concrete cases; it simply strengthens our disposition to discriminate. Prudence and justice allow us to determine innocence in war, while love impels us to act upon that knowledge.

As a matter of justice we cannot formulate war-fighting strategies whose success depends upon the killing of innocent people. To target innocent lives deliberately and as a necessary feature of a winning strategy shows both a wrong intention as the reason for fighting as well as a violation of the guideline of noncombatant immunity.

(This discrimination and immunity does not apply, however, to soldiers killing soldiers. The pacifist Hauerwas argues that just warriors "can never kill gladly"; moreover, "the Christian soldier should not intend to kill the enemy but rather seek only to incapacitate him so as to prevent him from achieving his purpose."[1] This, however, is a misapplication of just war doctrine.)

THE QUESTION OF INTENTION

Regrettably, innocent people are likely to be killed even in a just war, but the justice of a war is not *necessarily* compromised when the innocent are killed; we must first ask if those deaths were intentional.

In an often quoted passage of the *Summa Theologica*, Aquinas argued that "nothing hinders one act from having two effects, only one of which is intended, while the other is beside the intention" (II-II.64.7). Aquinas went on to show how killing someone in self-defense is acceptable, so long as you intended only to defend yourself.

When Aquinas spoke of this double effect of an action, he did not mean that we can channel our intention in a certain way in order to make *any* act seem just. Someone who beats a child to death with a steel pipe might defend his action by saying that while he was hitting the child his intention was directed entirely upon exercising his arm muscles, and he did not actually "intend" to harm the child. This is the same sort of approach to intention held by certain infamous Jesuits savaged by Pascal in his *Provincial Letters*.

In understanding actual intention, Aquinas stressed the importance of what someone actually *does*. Roughly speaking, what you did is what you actually intended, and what matters most are the observable circumstances. The most important circumstance of human actions is the *why*. When you fully answer the question of why you did something, you have a good idea what your intention was. When we choose to act in a certain way, we choose to do so for some goal.

The appropriateness of applying such analysis to just actions in proper just war is obvious. Do the combat actions in question contain elements of callousness, intemperance, impatience, or cruelty? Was this particular action the only way to achieve the good in this instance? Was this act the only way to secure peace, or to punish evildoers, or to uplift the good? Such questions come into play when we render a verdict on intention.

After a bombing mission in which civilians nearby were killed, a pilot might explain the mission by saying, "By bombing this railroad depot in the middle of the city, what was intended was both to weaken the enemy's supply lines *and* to demoralize the civilian population by causing civilian casualties." In that case, the standard of noncombatant immunity has been violated.

Or the pilot might say that nothing more was intended by the attack than to destroy the transportation of enemy munitions and troops to the front line. Although the pilot and those who planned his mission knew that in the course of destroying the depot, civilian deaths were not unlikely, they did not intend those deaths.

Another way of looking at this is to ask, Would this mission have been carried out even if no innocent people were nearby? Did the presence of innocent people in or near the depot serve no part in the attackers' motivation or reasons to bomb the target? The pilot and the planners of the mission, if just, will not wish to kill innocent people, and they will wish that there were no innocent civilians in or near any area that they must attack.

We can ask other questions as well in looking for traces of vice in the way the bombing mission was formed and carried out: Are the leaders patient in their pursuit of victory in this war? Have they consistently avoided trying to "get back" at the enemy by striking terror into civilians? Were the leaders sufficiently careful in planning the bombing run in order to avoid, as much as possible, injury or death to civilians? Was the pilot sufficiently careful in dropping his bombs? (Recklessness by the pilot would be the same as recklessness in driving on crowded city streets. A reckless driver who kills or injures others will be charged with a crime, and it's the same kind of crime to be reckless in bombing tactics.)

If all these questions can be answered positively, we have good reasons for supposing the intention to be good on the part of those who planned and carried out the bombing mission. The important point is that we do not determine this merely by asking the pilot and mission planners to report their intentions but also through observation of their actions.

In our example of innocent deaths in the depot bombing, some will feel it is rather specious reasoning that allows us to say such deaths are "unintended." If we know civilian deaths are likely from a planned military action, is that really any different from deliberately intending those deaths? Isn't it true that to know (foresee) is to intend? William V. O'Brien, for example, has argued that if an attacker "knows that there are noncombatants intermingled with combatants to the point that any attack on the military target is highly likely to kill or injure noncombatants, then the death or injury to those noncombatants is certainly 'intended' or 'deliberately willed' in the common usage of those words."[2] In *Force, Order, and Justice,* Robert Osgood and Robert Tucker assumed O'Brien's definition of intention, then concluded that discrimination can in no way be reconciled to modern warfare.[3]

The mistake these authors make is a failure to understand how we can foresee something but not intend it. For example, as a teacher I can foresee that when I give students bad grades, they'll be angry. But it would be a mistake to think I *intend* to make them angry by giving bad grades. Likewise, we can foresee that certain acts of force will kill innocent people without intending those deaths.

PROPORTION

One further thing must be settled before we could judge whether bombing the railroad depot is just or unjust. We would have to examine this action under the *jus in bello* criterion of proportion. Does the intended good (elimination of the depot) outweigh the potential consequence of the innocents killed?

Prudence is the virtue that helps us arrive at an answer, and the fact that there's no hard and fast rule for such cases is no argument against pursuing this virtue. There's no chart to consult that will tell us a military depot of such and such a size can be destroyed as long as the projected loss of innocent life does not exceed a certain number. Our only hope for acting rightly in such circumstances is to exercise prudence in weighing the likely success of the mission (destroying the depot) against the mission's positive effect (debilitating enemy power) and negative effect (killing innocents).

Exercising this prudence is the responsibility of each individual warrior and also their commanders, and none of them attains this prudence without the grace of God and the skill learned through training and practice under master warriors. The virtuous commander knows when and with how much force to attack. Like most knowledge in skillful practice, this becomes habitual, though it still at times requires deliberation.

When we decide on a fighting strategy, we must calculate to the best of our ability the risks of unintended results such as the deaths of civilians. If our strategy demands, even indirectly, the lives of too many innocent people, we have to create another strategy.

JUDGING WAR CRIMES

Standards for proper combat behavior go beyond the just war doctrine of *jus in bello*. These numerous standards go back to ancient codes of war and still exist in current international laws governing war, such as the series of international agreements known as the Hague and Geneva Conventions. Violations of these codes can lead to prosecutions for war crimes.

No doubt the most famous war crimes trials were those held at Nuremberg between November 1945 and October 1946. The Nuremberg Tribunal heard the cases of a number of Nazi leaders charged with three sorts of crimes: (1) crimes against peace, (2) war crimes, and (3) crimes against humanity. The crimes against humanity concerned the treatment of nonmilitary personnel, especially the Jews. The overriding crime was that of aggressive war—a direct violation of international law and the traditional *jus ad bellum*. Germany had started a war for which there was no just cause. According to the American prosecutor, Germany's aggression "was a war in violation of treaties by which the peace of the world was sought to be safeguarded."[4]

As a result of the Tribunal's conviction of their atrocities, German high commanders Keitel and Jodl were hanged, 24 other Nazis were executed, and another 114 were imprisoned. Thirty-five were acquitted.

Less famous were war crimes trials held in Tokyo for the major war criminals in the Pacific conflict. The Allies tried 5,000 Japanese and executed 900, many for their mistreatment of Allied prisoners of war. The following is from an account of a

British officer taken prisoner; it is by no means an uncommon account:

> I was called forward. I stood to attention. [The guards] stood facing me, breathing heavily. There was a pause. It seemed to drag on for minutes. Then I went down with a blow that shook every bone, and which released a sensation of scorching liquid pain which seared through my entire body. Sudden blows struck me all over. I felt myself plunging downwards into an abyss.... I could identify the periodic stamping of boots on the back of my head, crunching my face into the gravel; the crack of bones snapping; my teeth breaking; and my own involuntary attempts to respond to deep vicious kicks and to regain an upright position, only to be thrown to the ground once more.
>
> At one point I realized that my hips were being damaged and I remember looking up and seeing pick-helves coming down toward my hips, and putting my arms in the way to deflect the blows. This seemed only to focus the clubs on my arms and hands.... Yet the worse pain came from the pounding on my pelvic bones and the base of my spine. I think they tried to smash my hips. My whole trunk was brutally defined for me, like having my skeleton etched out in pain....

I do know that I thought I was dying. I have
never forgotten, from that moment onwards, crying out "Jesus," crying out for help, the utter
despair of helplessness. I rolled into a deep ditch
of foul stagnant water which, in the second or
two before consciousness was finally extinguished,
flowed over me with the freshness of a pure and
sweet spring.[5]

It requires a great deal of grace not to view these prison guards
as irrational animals fit only to be caught and killed. Prisoners are
by definition helpless people who can pose no threat and are not
proper targets for violence. Certainly they may be kept imprisoned, but they may not be tortured. Torture is not justice. Torture
is evil.

War crimes trials nevertheless often seem to us as something
less than worthy or appropriate. Our culture's moral relativism,
combined with the cynical view that justice is in the hands of the
winner, leads many to think that what we get in a war crimes trial
is the justice of hypocritical winners meted out to the unfortunate
losers.

We've often heard others say, "What's morally good for me
may be morally bad for you. No one should judge another by his
own personal morality." The argument is popular in discussions on
every moral issue imaginable: "I personally would never have an
abortion or have sex with someone of the same gender, but I'm
unwilling to tell others these things are wrong for them. I won't
impose my morality on someone else."

With the prevalence of such thinking, you can see the difficulty in war crimes trials already. If we cannot impose morality on another individual, how can we impose it on another nation? In the eyes of such people, war crimes trials are merely a power play by the victorious side of the conflict. It's only another case of might makes right, or as the ancient philosopher Thrasymachus said in one of Plato's dialogues, "Justice is the interests of the stronger" (*Republic* I).

Relativist moral thinking is so ingrained in our culture that I once witnessed a young Jewish man admit he had no real moral grounds for condemning Nazi atrocities against the Jews, because such blame arose from a "parochial" morality that could not be universalized; he could not impose his own morality onto the Nazis. When we ask such people why we should have any laws at all, they usually respond that laws are a particular people's way of protecting themselves and allowing their own society to run smoothly. Such laws should not be imposed on those who aren't a member of that particular society. Criminal trials for violating supposedly universal standards of warfare conduct would therefore be impossible, or at least hypocritical, because they would impose morality on those who do not wish to play by another society's rules.

Christians, however, believe that God gave human beings a universal moral law that must be obeyed by all peoples at all times and in all places. The Ten Commandments are a perfect summation of this moral law, whose requirements are also "written in the hearts" of all human beings (Romans 2:15). The Christian just war doctrine is an attempt to extrapolate from God's moral law a moral approach to using force on earth. Those who violate just war stand-ards are guilty of moral offense before mankind and before God, and it is right that they should have to answer to any nation or nations that enforce those standards. They will also, of course, have to answer to God, but that is another story.

CHAPTER SIX

World War II, Vietnam, and the Gulf War

Applying Just War Analysis

We judge a tool's usefulness in proportion to how well it performs the task it's designed to perform. We call a knife good in proportion to how well it cuts. We call a drill good in proportion to how well it drills. The just war doctrine represents a tool for Christians, allowing them to figure out the justice of a war, and it can be judged a good tool in proportion to how well it reveals the justice or injustice of war.

In this chapter we'll use just war criteria to examine World War II, the Vietnam conflict, and the 1991 Gulf War. You won't find here an exhaustive moral analysis of the causes of each conflict or of how it was fought; each of those subjects would require its own book, if not its own set of volumes. Instead, we'll try to suggest how the just war criteria work in practice by examining key moral issues in each conflict. By seeing the just war doctrine "in action," we'll be able to determine how useful a tool it is for Christians.

WORLD WAR II

In an essay at the onset of World War II titled "The Justice of the Present War Examined," G. E. M. Anscombe, a student at Oxford and later a noted English philosopher, worried that the Allied war aims were unjust because they included the stipulation of unconditional surrender, a goal that could cause the war to become especially vicious and cruel.

As subsequent events proved, Anscombe's fears were well founded. In a later essay, "Mr. Truman's Degree," Anscombe looked back on the war and reasonably concluded that the insistence on unconditional surrender was "the root of all evil" in the conflict, at least on the side of the Allies; it led to the "most ferocious methods of warfare."[1] In Japan, for example, neither a mass Allied invasion nor the use of atomic weapons might have been needed had the Allies formulated a viable plan of conditional surrender.

Our look at World War II through the grid of the just war doctrine will focus on the issues involved in the saturation bombing of enemy cities, including the atomic bombs dropped on Japanese cities, which brought the war to an end.

SATURATION BOMBING

Let's begin our discussion by clarifying a few terms. *Precision bombing* is for definite, limited military targets, such as airfields, ammo dumps, railroad depots, and so forth. *Saturation* or *obliteration bombing* targets not a well-defined military objective but an entire city or section of a city (including large residential areas). The purpose of obliteration bombing is to terrorize and thus demoralize innocent civilians of an enemy nation.

In the early days of the war, the British did not make use of obliteration bombing. In fact, Winston Churchill in 1940 condemned Germany's policy of indiscriminate bombing on London as a "new and odious form of warfare."

Soon, however, Churchill was telling the public that to win the war, there was no limit to the violence the Allies would consider using. In 1942, with the appointment of Sir Arthur Travers Harris to the control of Bomber Command, the RAF began to practice obliteration bombing. Major General Clarence Eaker, commander of the United States Eighth Air Force, was Harris's partner in the new policy.

Because of their advanced bombsights, Americans carried out the daytime precision bombing while the British carried out obliteration bombing by night. Nevertheless, Americans also sometimes participated in the night raids, and American leaders helped formulate the overall bombing strategy.

According to those in charge, the bombing of Germany had two main objectives: (1) the destruction of Germany's major industrial cities, and (2) the destruction of all military factories, railroads, and communications in general. The war planners made it quite clear that they intended to wipe out residential districts where workers lived with their families. Many of these raids, purposely aimed at residential districts, killed thousands of civilian men, women, and children.

Leaders in the United States approved of the bombings. President Roosevelt defended obliteration bombing on the grounds that it would shorten the war. In the official American military publication *Target: Germany,* the writer makes clear that the terrorization of civilians was part of the bombing strategy: "The physical attrition of warfare is no longer limited to the fighting forces."[2] The purpose was to undermine the morale of the enemy by injuring and killing civilians.

CONSEQUENTIALISM

Behind such thinking is the moral philosophy of consequentialism—the approach that the end justifies the means. For G. E. M. Anscombe, the philosopher who early on expressed doubt about the goal of unconditional surrender, such consequentialism is a chief complaint about modern moral philosophy; philosophers construct theories of ethics that may be formally beautiful, but in the end these systems always allow someone to commit dreadful acts in the name of moral correctness.

Anscombe's fears have been amply borne out with respect to just war thinking. The most influential study of the just war doctrine in the last twenty years[3] is a work that justifies the use of morally vicious actions for a good end: Michael Walzer's *Just and Unjust Wars.*[4]

Walzer's use of the concept of "supreme emergency" exemplifies consequentialist thinking. In a nutshell, Walzer argued that if we're faced with the complete collapse of civilization as we know it—if, for example, a nation like Nazi Germany is on the verge of taking over our world—then *no* actions taken against such an evil power could be described as morally wrong. The historical example Walzer employed is the Allied decision to use saturation bombing on German cities in World War II.

Although saturation bombing is inherently unjust—innocent civilians were deliberately and willingly slaughtered; part of the very purpose of saturation bombing was to kill enough innocent civilians to demoralize the enemy—Walzer said it was the necessary thing to do to ensure the survival of the anti-Nazi West. "Necessity knows no rules," as he aptly put it.

No attempt was made to portray such bombing as honorable. In fact, Walzer pointed out with satisfaction how British Air Marshall Arthur Harris (the brain behind saturation bombing) was not honored by Churchill after the war, and hence was effectively dishonored. Harris, nevertheless, arguably made Allied victory possible[5] and was therefore engaged in what Walzer viewed as acceptable action—morally right—in a time of "supreme emergency."

APPLYING THE TESTS OF DISCRIMINATION AND PROPORTIONALITY

The term *noncombatant* once included all who did not bear arms, but modern industrial war has clouded the issue of who are the actual combatants. Some go so far as to argue that modern industrial cities are themselves legitimate battlefields and that everyone living in an industrial city is a combatant.

"To-day everyone is a military person," Karl Barth wrote, "either directly or indirectly. That is to say, everyone participates in the suffering and action which war demands."[6] This statement is worse than nonsense—it's the sort of nonsense that leads to great moral evil. For if every person is a "military person," then every person is a legitimate target, and the just war criterion of discrimination—noncombatant immunity—is completely emptied of application.

Think about what this means. Every man, woman, and child, regardless of physical and mental capacity, regardless of their role in society, is a proper target. While it's true that civilian munitions workers or members of organized labor battalions may constitute a gray area in our evaluation, not everything (or everyone) is gray. A common fallacy is to argue that because there's a gray area, we should drop moral principles altogether, as if there were *no* white or black areas to which our principles could clearly apply. This is clearly wrong.

We also must apply the *jus in bello* standard of proportionality to obliteration bombing. Did we expect the good of this bombing to outweigh the evil? Did it actually shorten the war? Many military leaders doubted it at the time. Moreover, even if obliteration bombing did shorten the war, and even if it did save military lives, we still have to consider what the result for the future would be if this way of doing war were made generally legitimate. The immediate result was to combine obliteration bombing strategy with nuclear weapons as a way to threaten the annihilation of whole nations.

THE ATOMIC BOMBS

As a replacement strategy for the mass land invasion of Japan, the use of atomic weapons on Hiroshima and Nagasaki certainly saved thousands of Allied lives, and perhaps even thousands of Japanese lives, especially given the fact that the Allies would accept no terms of surrender short of complete capitulation.

In a book with a lead essay titled "Thank God for the Atom Bomb," just war critic Paul Fussell argues that war is a nasty business that should be brought to an end as speedily as possible; insofar as the atomic attacks on Hiroshima and Nagasaki accomplished this task, they were the right thing to do.[7]

Fussell lists eight reasons why America did the right thing in dropping atomic weapons on Japan. They represent most of the reasons we usually hear, so it would be helpful to list them. Following each one, in italics, is the sort of response the just war defender might make.

1. In the event of a mass land invasion of Japan, at least one million American casualties were expected, not to mention thousands of British casualties. (John Kenneth Galbraith claimed that Japan would have surrendered even if the Allies had not mounted a land invasion, and that the atomic bombs hastened the war's end by only two or three weeks. Even then, some fourteen to twenty-one thousand American casualties could be expected during those weeks of delay. As Fussell says,

"Those weeks meant the world if you're one of those thousands or related to one of them."[8])

We must be willing to die justly and honorably rather than to live unjustly and cowardly. The just war doctrine says that we must not do evil that good might result.

2. Fussell notes that Japan did not seek peace until after a second bomb was dropped on Nagasaki, and that Japan, prior to the bombings, had announced that women from the ages of seventeen to forty were being enlisted to repel any land invasion. This speaks volumes against any claims of an imminent surrender.

This logic only works because the Allies sought an unconditional surrender. Terms of an unconditional surrender tend to lead to unlimited war aims, which in turn, tend to give rise to a sense of purposelessness that breeds all sorts of vicious and unacceptable behavior. In any event, it's always wrong to kill innocent people as a means to an end. The very fact that the Allies intended the deaths of innocent civilians makes the bombing of Hiroshima and Nagasaki an act dangerously close to mass murder.

3. Fussell quotes one intelligence officer as saying, "There are no civilians in Japan." Because of full-scale mobiliza-

tion, the entire population was perceived as a proper military target.

Even if Japan had mobilized every available person, the unavailable—small children, the sick, the aged, the mentally retarded—would still have to be considered noncombatants. Literally speaking, there is no such thing as a "nation at arms."

4. The use of atomic weapons was seen as merely a continuation of previous Allied policy. The Allies had been killing Japanese civilians for some time, and there was no special reason to be ashamed of using atomic bombs to continue doing so (although apparently some American military personnel felt differently[9]).

Fussell is referring, of course, to the "barbaric" practice (to use General Patton's term) of bombing the centers of cities such as Dresden and Tokyo. Nevertheless, the fact that we have acted unjustly in the past is no justification for continuing to do so.

5. Hiroshima and Nagasaki were properly and mainly military targets. It is often overlooked that ten thousand Japanese troops were among the dead in Hiroshima and Nagasaki.

*This is as close as Fussell comes to making a successful jus-
tification. Because Hiroshima and Nagasaki were legitimate military targets, the Allied purpose in dropping the
bombs was not purely "terroristic." But the question of
proportion comes into play, and one would have a hard
time making a case that the overall good outweighed the
overall evil.*

6. Through leaflets dropped on the target cities, fair warning was given to civilians there before the bombings.
   There would be no reason to drop all those leaflets if our
   purpose was merely to slaughter thousands of innocents.

   *Giving fair warning to the citizens does not make everything
   morally acceptable. If I hit someone over the head with a
   brick, my guilt for that action isn't removed if I warned him
   about it beforehand.*

7. Antibomb sentiments are partly due to the igno-
   rance of Japanese atrocities. Fussell says the Japanese
   were particularly sadistic in their combat behavior,
   and that Americans would not be so ready to condemn the use of the atomic bomb if they were more
   familiar with how horribly the Japanese treated the Allies.

   *Fussell's justification seems rather to condemn Americans
   in general, and war leaders in particular, for their inability*

*to refrain from overly harsh reprisals against Japanese
atrocities. As Fussell himself admits, the Americans
were "irrationally remembering Pearl Harbor with a
vengeance."*[10]

8. Soldiers cannot be expected to be "sensitive humanitarians," since they spend so much time in kill-or-be-killed situations. It's natural for them to want to end the war as quickly as possible, regardless of how the end is accomplished.

    *This is more an assessment of the kind of soldier our society
    spawns than a moral justification for dropping atomic
    bombs. I hope Fussell's assessment is wrong, but if it's true
    that we do not produce humanitarian soldiers, it's because
    we've chosen not to do so. Christians cannot be happy
    about that.*

In summary, the Second World War was a just war, but because the Allies' war aims were tainted (through being unlimited), this led to moral evils such as indiscriminate bombing and other tactics that were defended as doing the lesser evil for the greater good.

The just war criterion of right intention demands limited war aims for a just cause. Had the Allies adhered to this criterion, perhaps a great deal of moral evil could have been avoided. Perhaps we would have realized that it's better to be killed by Nazis than to act like Nazis, for if we allow warfare to reduce us to acting like Nazis, what's the point of the war? Wasn't it fought in order to preserve a way of life that prohibits things like killing innocent people deliberately and intentionally?

None of this is to deny the overall justice of World War II. Those who died in the war to preserve the Western way of life are truly heroes. But to command moral evil, as some war leaders did, is not a heroic act.

VIETNAM

Trying to explain the Vietnam conflict, let alone trying to analyze the morality of its war aims, is a full-time job that has yet to be completed by any historian with total objectivity. Vietnam is still a lightning rod that divides historians, ethicists, and just about everyone else.

Let's set before us a few clear historical facts. In Indochina, from 1941 to 1954, communist Vietnamese forces fought a revolutionary war against French colonial forces. The United States supported the French effort to "contain communism" in Southeast Asia by supplying the French forces with arms.

When the French realized that there was no way to win the war (or that the war was not worth winning—pick your historian), they agreed to partition Vietnam, and French troops were withdrawn in 1954. The United States continued to support the anticommunist government of South Vietnam against the communist regime in the North. This support began with arms and military advisors; later, several hundred thousand American troops were engaged.

Why did the United States care what would happen to a small country halfway around the world? American involvement in Vietnam can be understood only within the Cold War context. First, the "domino theory" held that if South Vietnam fell to communism, all of Southeast Asia would also fall in time. Second, the United States had to defend its credibility as a superpower; Americans could not let it appear that the Soviets, who were throwing all their support behind the communist regime in North Vietnam, could get the upper hand on the United States whenever they wanted it.

A JUST WAR?

Looking first at the *jus ad bellum* criteria, there was certainly proper authority for American involvement and, until the last days, a reasonable hope for success (although some historians put the final date for reasonable hope for success as early as 1964). Also, a good case can be made that the war was the only way to do justice in this case—assuming, of course, that the cause of defending South Vietnam was just.

That brings us to the most contentious issue. Did the United States have just cause and right intention in the Vietnam conflict? The answer depends largely on how we answer three prior questions: Was containing communism in Southeast Asia a just cause? Assuming it was a just cause, was containing communism in Southeast Asia worth the cost of a war? Finally, in pursuing this just cause, was South Vietnam the sort of state to which we should have pledged help?

Let's take the last question first. On the face of it, South Vietnam was not the sort of nation that the United States ought to have supported. The South Vietnamese government was corrupt to begin with, and it may have become even more corrupt while Americans were in the country.

In objection to this argument, some may note that the United States gave aid to Soviet Russia during World War II in order to defeat Nazi Germany. This was a case of supporting an evil regime for a good cause—so why not in Vietnam too? But this view of American support for the Soviets in World War II is only partially true, and even if entirely true, it would not be a good justification for American involvement in Vietnam.

The United States provided aid to Soviet Russia partly because doing so meant stalling Germany's plans for conquest and partly because our leaders were extremely naive about the nature of the communist regime in Russia. In hindsight, the Soviet Union and fascist Germany were both morally evil regimes that needed to be resisted. Such naiveté did not exist about South Vietnam; our knowledge of their government was quite good from the very beginning.

I wanted to answer the third question first, because, as you can probably guess by now, it helps us answer the other questions. Containing communism wasn't a bad idea, but it *was* a bad idea to do it by supporting another corrupt regime.

HOW JUSTLY DID AMERICANS FIGHT?

More troubling to most people is not so much the justice of the American cause in Vietnam, but the means used to pursue it (and to have had the bad grace to fail even at that).

The My Lai massacre is for many people the immoral exemplar of our tactics during the entire Vietnam conflict. This incident cannot be properly evaluated without some knowledge of the nature of the Americans' chief enemy, the Vietcong (communist rebels in South Vietnam who were supported by North Vietnam). The Vietcong employed guerrilla tactics that relied upon mobility and surprise attacks to wear down larger enemy forces. Guerrilla warriors are citizen soldiers who can fade into the general populace undetected by the enemy. (North Vietnam's National Liberation Front named its paramilitary forces *Don Quan,* which means "civilian soldiers," thus emphasizing that the army was indistinguishable from the civilian populace.) Naturally, such a strategy plays havoc with the *jus in bello* criterion of discrimination.

The Vietcong deliberately hid among the citizenry and used women and children in combat as a way to entice the United States to fire upon innocent civilians indiscriminately, and thus to get the populace on their side. The Vietcong created a "battlefield" where telling combatants apart from noncombatants was nearly impossible and where it was dangerous even to try.

In such circumstances, a great deal of leeway must be given even to those soldiers who "shoot first and ask questions later";

nevertheless, even in this extreme scenario, not everyone is a target all the time. Some discrimination could have been made but sometimes was not, as the My Lai massacre makes abundantly clear. At My Lai, scores of obviously innocent people were slaughtered. Some American soldiers, realizing that these "targets" were not soldiers of any kind, refused to continue with the slaughter. Theirs was the correct response, according to the Christian just war tradition.

THE GULF WAR

The American military learned a lot from the Vietnam experience, especially about the public perception of how a war is fought. A new emphasis on precise targeting and the determination to kill as few innocent people as possible—and none intentionally—marked the new approach taken in the Persian Gulf War in 1990–1991.

Americans tend to have a hard time fighting limited wars. When we think our cause just, our immediate reaction is to want to obliterate absolutely. (After the 2001 terrorist attacks on the World Trade Center and the Pentagon, and the identification of Afghanistan as the center of the terrorists' network, the common refrain that dinned in my ears was, "Let's nuke the whole country.") A crusade mentality and the kind of fighting that goes with it have too often been the ugly badges of American war fighting. But the Gulf War provided a refreshing example of American willingness to fight justly for limited aims.

When looking at the events leading up to the war, it must be pointed out that America (and the West in general) had supported Saddam Hussein during the 1980s for a variety of reasons, most notably the fear of Iran. America supplied Hussein with arms to fight Iran and taught Hussein's administration how to use chemical and biological weapons. Already we find ourselves on shaky moral ground. The United States was helping an unjust regime with efforts to use inherently unjust weapons, for chemical and biological weapons are notoriously indiscriminate. Nevertheless, this troubling background doesn't mean that America was necessarily immoral in opposing Iraq when Iraq unjustly invaded Kuwait and began to commit atrocities.

America and much of the West responded to this unjust aggression for reasons that were both altruistic and self-interested. We should find nothing troubling about that fact; there's nothing wrong with a state acting in its own self-interests as long as those interests are lawful.

What were America's self-interests, and how were they pursued in the Gulf War? American self-interest in the Middle East is largely confined to oil production. Americans consume a lot of oil and don't want to pay a lot for it. This is not in itself unlawful; everyone wants goods at the cheapest price possible. But is keeping our current supply of oil at the status quo level a sufficient cause for going to war?

Another leading cause of the Gulf War was the fear of Iraq's increasing capabilities to commit further injustices with biological, chemical, and nuclear weapons. Hussein was doing terrible things to his neighbors, and he was developing the capabilities to do even worse things. This in itself constituted a good enough reason to fight Iraq. Kuwait might not have been a neighbor worthy of significant American support, but the same cannot be said about the entire Middle East, especially the state of Israel, which likely would have been one of the prime targets for Hussein's growing capacities for unjust fighting.

After Iraq's aggression, Western powers responded first with siege and embargo tactics. The justice of such tactics is itself a cause for concern. Siege and embargo tactics strike at the innocent as much as the guilty. The UN sanctions allowed food and medical supplies to be brought in, but the innocent still suffered to a great degree. (By early December 1990, the Iraqi health minister claimed that fourteen hundred children had died; a UN study conducted after the hostilities ceased estimated that seventy thousand people—most of them innocent—had died as a result of the sanctions.)

Gulf War critics such as Kenneth Vaux have argued that the siege should have been given at least nine months to work,[11] but he fails to take into account that Iraq had occupied a nation unjustly; it was not simply a matter of neutralizing the enemy inside Iraq but of rescuing Kuwait.

So the air attack on Iraq and the rescue of Kuwait began. As to the justice of the fighting done in the war, little needs to be said. The Gulf War was one of the most cleanly fought modern wars on record, which is not to say that the Gulf War record is without blemish. American troops carpet-strafed helpless retreating Iraqis who were obviously posing no further threat. But such incidents were isolated, and this makes all the difference. No inherently unjust tactics were carried out as a matter of routine practice during the Gulf War.

CHAPTER SEVEN

Nuclear Weapons and Deterrence

Restoring the Ability to Fight Justly

S trategies for using nuclear weapons derive from the World War II doctrine of obliteration bombing, where the goal was to attack large areas of cities or even entire cities. Remembering the shock of being hit with a first-strike surprise attack by the Japanese at Pearl Harbor, certain American strategists insisted on the doctrine of the vital first blow with nuclear weapons.

While strategically sound, the moral consequences of striking first with nuclear weapons made this tactic unpopular. Nevertheless, a strategy emerged in which preemptive strikes (a first strike that prevents an enemy from striking us) were possible.

More attractive morally speaking was a strategy for retaliatory strikes. This move from first strike to retaliation gave the United States a capacity for deterrence but not the capacity to win a military victory. Thus nuclear weapons became useful for deterrence only.

This is an important point: Nuclear weapons were considered useful for deterring others from attacking us but not for actual use. If the United States actually has to use nuclear weapons, those weapons fail in their purpose. So "the basic axioms of the nuclear age" (as Lawrence Freedman calls them) were in place by the late 1940s: "the impossibility of defense; the hopeless vulnerability of the world's major cities; the attraction of sudden attack; and the necessity for retaliation."[1]

The entire history of American nuclear strategy is the story behind the battle fought between those who were comfortable with these axioms and those who wished to break away—between those who wished to rely on weapons so awful in their capabilities that we could not possibly use them and those who wished to rely on less lethal weapons that could be used without threatening the annihilation of the entire world.

As previously noted, nuclear weapons strategies from the very beginning were based on the World War II doctrine of obliteration bombing—a doctrine that we have seen is immoral by Christian just war standards. Obliteration bombing, however, was not without its military critics even in World War II. Many war leaders argued that indiscriminate bombing of cities did little to win the war and that only the destruction of industrial targets proved effective. This early notion of limited warfare in the face of modern total war provides the seeds for those strategists uncomfortable with the basic axioms of the nuclear age.

One of those dissatisfied with the axioms, Walter Lippmann, argued that America had found its wish fulfillment in the atom bomb and that this indicated a moral failure—that the

United States was not morally prepared to fight a just war. Possessing such terrible weapons, the American threat was simple: If you launch a direct attack on the United States, we will obliterate your country.

The basic axioms of the nuclear age support deterrent strategy over retaliation strategy. Dissatisfied with this, some strategists began to ask, "What if it becomes necessary to actually retaliate? What if deterrence fails?" Herman Kahn, for example, argued for more military preparedness for such a possibility and said that to ignore such a strategy "borders on the irresponsible."[2] His stated goal was to fight and survive. Critics of Kahn argued that Soviet nuclear capabilities made such a war inconceivable. The Soviets had the capability to launch so many missiles at us at one time that any talk of "survival" was meaningless.

It was estimated that a nuclear exchange between the United States and the Soviet Union, with strikes against military objectives only, would have resulted in the deaths of between 35–77 percent of the U.S. population. If ballistic missiles were fired on nonmilitary targets as well, as many as 30 million additional people would have been killed. These are the realities of nuclear destruction.

The United States may no longer face the active hostility of the former Soviet Union with its nuclear capabilities, but it could still be hit with a solitary nuclear weapon from another enemy. While such an attack would not mean the end of America's existence as a nation, it's still a terrible thing to contemplate. Solly Zuckerman pointed out how the destruction perpetrated by even a one-megaton hydrogen bomb over a modern European or American city would be enormous and would "almost inevitably lead to its total elimination."[3] Moreover, an enemy with better capabilities would probably target multiple cities.

The Cold War was marked by a stalemate in which both the Americans and the Soviets had become sophisticated enough with their weapons technologies that there was no way to outdistance each other with new weapons. Thus we entered the age of mutually assured destruction (MAD). Any use of nuclear weapons by either superpower meant the total obliteration of both powers, and quite possibly the rest of the world as well. Of course, many believed that this was precisely this awful possibility that kept the superpowers from actually attacking one another.

In the midst of these Cold War realities, the ability to wage conventional war was not completely abandoned, and continuing efforts over the years were made by some strategists to turn things around.

Those who support nuclear deterrence can honestly claim that it worked insofar as the United States and the Soviet Union never engaged in nuclear exchanges. But outside of the two-superpowers model, there is no reason to assume that America's present deterrence policy will continue working. What worked against the former Soviet Union may not work against North Korea or China or Iraq. In a world where there are no longer two superpowers playing the deterrence game, it's time to rethink American deterrence policy.

EXPLORING ALTERNATIVES

Although the stated American goal for many years in nuclear policy has been to "keep our options open," the United States has made it clear that, under certain conditions, it will retaliate. Thus, America's present deterrence strategy is immoral by Christian just war standards.

Deterrence, however, is not intrinsically evil; there may be a just deterrence. But such a deterrence must meet two conditions: (1) Only enemy military forces are threatened, and (2) other potential deaths are accepted only as side effects (in other words, civilian casualties play no part in the intention).

According to Walzer, the basic form of nuclear deterrence is simple, if unjust: Against a threat of an immoral attack from our enemies, we have placed the threat of an immoral response. As it stands, two alternatives seem to face us: Threaten to kill millions of innocent people indiscriminately, or put ourselves at the mercy of an enemy nation.

The only way to make our response moral, and thus to get out of the dilemma, is to make effective threats with usable weapons. The argument is that while massive retaliation can have no rational purpose (though it may be rational to threaten it), a limited nuclear strike could serve a rational purpose. In limited strikes, the goal is to knock out military forces, not civilian populations; therefore, the requirements of the *jus in bello* are not violated.

Unfortunately, this strategy fails in two ways. First, proportion could never be satisfied, for the number of innocent people killed would trump any military advantage. Second, the threat of escalation would be too great. Of course, these two objections probably rule out large-scale conventional war as well.

So the dilemma remains: "Nuclear weapons are politically and militarily unusable only because and insofar as we can plausibly threaten to use them in some ultimate way. And it is immoral to make threats of that kind."[4]

But what if civilian deaths played no part in the intention? Proportion says that the intended good cannot be outweighed by the unintended evil of our means. If the intended good is to save our civilization, and the means includes a strike on or near a major enemy city where missiles are about to be launched against us, then there's no reason to assume out of hand that the strike is unjustified. Millions of innocent civilians might be killed, but we might save just as many, if not more, of our own innocent civilians, and perhaps preserve our civilization as a whole.

In that scenario, civilian casualties play no part in our intention. Again, going back to our discussion of intention, when we ask *why* we attack and *why* we use the means we do, the answer is that we attack to preserve ourselves, and nuclear weapons are the only means available to do so. Civilian deaths have no effect at all on our purposes or actions. We would have responded with the same strategic attack whether or not any civilians were near the target.

This scenario is, I believe, sound as far as it goes, but, unfortunately, it may not go very far. The threat of escalation hangs over any use of nuclear weapons. Furthermore, we have to remember that a death foreseen but not intended can still amount to murder if the action demonstrates reckless behavior. The risks of escalation are so great in any use of nuclear weapons that to use them in however small and limited a strike may evidence reckless behavior. I say "may" here, for it's impossible to know in advance all the circumstances surrounding a proposed conflict. Suffice it to say that we must keep the possible consequences in mind.

All we've established so far is that nuclear weapons may possibly be used justly; it may be hard to think of a concrete example, but, theoretically anyway, it may be possible to use low-yield, high-precision nuclear weapons.

There's one case that seems ripe for such use—a scenario too hastily dismissed by some. It's known as a *victory-denying strategy*, and it seeks to impose military losses on an enemy severe enough to impair the enemy's strategic goals. This is a response strategy that merely prevents an enemy from subsequent conquests. In *Nuclear Deterrence, Morality, and Realism,* authors Finnis, Boyle, and Grisez have argued that such a policy is in defiance of international law, which holds that all first strikes are illegal.[5] Yet victory-denying strategy comes into play only after an enemy has attacked us. The war, it would seem, has already been initiated, and we simply respond in such a way that we deny the enemy his ultimate goals, thus preventing a complete enemy victory.

Such a strategy seems entirely in accordance with traditional just war theory. True, we must not forget the criterion of reasonable hope of success, but success does not always mean complete military victory. Success in victory-denying strategy means that we deny the enemy a victory.

Victory-denying capability with low-yield, high-precision nuclear weapons should not stand alone. Conventional forces still would be needed, for two reasons. First, as Zuckerman has argued, conventional forces supplement nuclear forces in order to give a flexible-response ability (so that we aren't left with a "nuclear war or nothing" scenario). Second, conventional forces must constitute the means of our actual war-winning strategy.

This is not to imply that we're to build up our conventional forces in order to place ourselves in a better position to launch an attack, but rather, we are to defend ourselves with the goal of winning a conflict and not merely denying an enemy a victory in our death throes.

An arms race might be the immediate result of such a conventional forces buildup, but as bad as a new arms race might be, it is preferable to racing with weapons we cannot possibly use. Also, we must remind ourselves that the political climate is ripe for such a move. No longer are we faced with a huge, overpowering enemy. The reversion to conventional arms in the present climate would not amount to a vast buildup so much as a redirection in the kinds of arms that are needed for the new kinds of situations we might face.

One last note on conventional forces: Conventional weapons are not just weapons because they are conventional rather than nuclear; they are just weapons only insofar as they can be used with discrimination. The goal is to be able to fight justly. Research and development, therefore, should not be directed toward non-nuclear technologies that are indiscriminate.

On the basis of the previous arguments, the following position may bring nuclear deterrence into closer conformity with just war doctrine:

1. We should renounce all intentions for a war-winning nuclear strategy.
2. We should announce our intentions of a victory-denying nuclear strategy.
3. We should stop developing new indiscriminate nuclear technologies.

4. We should dismantle our current indiscriminate nuclear arsenal.

5. We should redirect research and development into giving low-yield nuclear weapons the greatest accuracy.

6. Conventional forces should be strengthened and reoriented to serve the goals previously mentioned.

These recommendations retain a certain amount of deterrence capability and give us the ability to fight justly.

CONCLUSION

Christians who adhere to their traditional just war doctrine cannot support the current U.S. deterrence policy, which threatens to kill millions of innocent people. Christians who follow Ambrose, Augustine, Aquinas, and Calvin should choose rather to suffer at the hands of an enemy than intentionally to kill innocent people.

One might respond that this deterrence policy is itself a work of love—a love of fellow American citizens—since this threat to kill thousands or even millions of innocent people is averting a catastrophe for America. Moreover, how can this be different from killing thousands of enemy soldiers and calling *that* a work of love?

The answer is simple: Enemy soldiers are not innocent civilians. We do no moral evil when we kill enemy soldiers in a just cause, but killing the innocent by the thousands, or even threatening to kill them by the thousands, is an immoral act in violation of the standard of love. We shouldn't need Ambrose, Augustine, Aquinas, or Calvin to tell us that.

CHAPTER EIGHT

Just Warfare and Terrorism

Facing a New Enemy

The terrorist attacks on the United States on September 11, 2001, have brought many people face-to-face with the fact of terrorism for the first time. Terrorism has been around for a long time, but, more than ever, people are beginning to question the morality of such actions.

First, let's get our facts straight. Terrorism has one purpose: to weaken the morale of a nation in order to move that attacked nation to desist in some activity that the terrorists perceive as harmful to them. The usual method employed is random murder of innocent civilians, though government and military targets can be attacked as well.

Few moralists wish to justify acts of terrorism. Michael Walzer, for example, devotes an entire chapter to denouncing the practice.[1] Walzer nevertheless is able to draw moral distinctions between an older form of terrorism found in the West in the early half of the twentieth century (exemplified by Russian revolutionaries, the IRA, and the Stern Group) and a newer form of terrorism found in the

East and Middle East in the last half of the century (exemplified by Mao Tse-tung, the Algerian FLN, and Muslim fundamentalists). Terrorists of the older form attacked people whom the accepted war convention usually protected—high-ranking government officials and politicians of regimes thought to be oppressive. But these terrorists often checked their acts of terrorism when innocent people could get killed. These terrorists still recognized that some acts of violence could not be carried out justly, and there was a recognized group of noncombatants. The distinguishing mark of the "newer" terrorism is that there is no such recognized group of noncombatants. For those who follow the teachings of Mao Tse-tung or Hamas, all members of an oppressive nation are legitimate targets.

Terrorists argue that attacks on civilians are justified by the principle of military necessity. The argument goes like this: "We, a just and oppressed people, cannot possibly defeat the oppressive nation that overwhelms us with military superiority. The only way we can become free is to use military tactics that will force the oppressors to quit oppressing us. If that means killing a lot of people whom our oppressors call 'innocent,' then so be it."

I remarked earlier that few moralists wish to defend terrorist attack, but we should not forget Cicero's famous remark that nothing is so foolish that some philosopher has not said it. Jean-Paul Sartre is the terrorist's philosopher. Sartre defended the FLN terrorists in Algeria with typically eloquent prose: "To shoot down a European is to kill two birds with one stone, to destroy an oppressor and the man he oppresses at the same time: there remains a dead man and a free man."[2] In other words, every time a terrorist kills a European—any European at all—that terrorist kills an oppressor and creates a free person. The argument is so obviously nonsense, even if we grant the premise that every European is responsible for oppressing some Algerian, that it's hard to believe an intelligent person said it. As Walzer points out, this perfect master-slave correlative does not exist in the real world. Not every European is an oppressive master. Yet Sartre could approve of the FLN killing even children in the name of freedom without making the slightest case for how children could oppress anyone. This is despicable moral reasoning, and Walzer is right to take Sartre to task for it.

Muslim terrorists are, perhaps, the most infamous terrorists of the last quarter century. Although the IRA has committed its recent share of unjust acts, Islamic fundamentalists have reached new heights of destruction. Yet even on most classical Islamic grounds, the actions of such terrorists are clearly unjust.

UNDERSTANDING CLASSICAL ISLAM AND WAR

We cannot possibly understand the terrorist acts of Muslim fundamentalists without first understanding something about classical Islamic approaches to war. Islam, like Christianity, has theological reasons for justifying the use of force when certain conditions are met. Also like Christianity, Islam has the ability to say no to some forms of conflict. But Islam and Christianity differ in crucial areas.

Religion and politics are interdependent in Islam; thus it is difficult to keep moral and religious justifications for war distinct. Nowhere is the problem more clearly evident than in how we are to understand the term *jihad*. The Koran uses two distinct terms for military activity—*qital,* which means "fighting," and *jihad,* which means "striving" (in the path of God). In the Koran, specific military activity is described using *qital* while *jihad* is used to describe the overall religious struggle. *Jihad* was used to describe specific military activity only after the first wave of huge successes in expanding the sphere of Islam *(dar al-Islam)* in the seventh century.

By the tenth century, *jihad* had come to mean any military action to expand the territory of Islam. The call to faith means a call to *jihad.* One is required to establish and maintain the sort of social order that will promote and protect the common good of the human community. The goal is to eradicate corruption on earth. Thus, the Koran justifies a defensive *jihad* that enjoins Muslims to fight those who stand in the way of God's cause on earth. But it also enjoins Muslims not merely to protect a just order on earth but to expand it to all people. Thus, offensive *jihad* may be justified as well.

According to traditional Muslim belief, human beings are responsible for a just social order. Similar to the teaching of Paul, this knowledge of a just social order is written on human hearts by God. But human beings forget or ignore this law.

The world is currently divided into two spheres. The sphere ruled by those who follow God's law is the territory of Islam *(dar al-Islam)*. The other sphere is the territory of war *(dar al-harb)*.

The just ruler must be capable of making judgments based on the Koran and the traditions. He must consult the religious authorities and protect their consensus, and he must support Islamic values.

Peace means work; it means *jihad*—struggle. One form of *jihad* is extending the territory of Islam with military force. For Muslim philosophers and theologians, the problem is how to distinguish between military operations that seek merely to expand territory for secular, imperial purposes, and military operations that seek to expand God's true religion. Most Sunni Muslims (who make up about 90 percent of all Muslims) agree that the conquests of the first two centuries following Muhammad were legitimate *jihad*, even though Shi'ites point out that God's true religion was not always spread with military power.

There are differences between Sunni and Shi'i perspectives on war. Sunni Muslims believe that right authority to lead *jihad* rests with any legitimate Muslim political leader, while Shi'ite Muslims believe that offensive *jihad* can be led only by a divinely appointed *Imam* (a charismatic leader). So Sunni Muslim scholars focus on providing a rationale for how the Sunni Muslim community has in fact acted in the world (through military expansion), while Shi'ites have always striven for the ideal. Both agree that wars of self-defense are obligatory, and both agree that only certain sorts of unbelievers are proper objects of attack—namely, those who show hostility to Islam by either persecuting Muslims or actively standing in the way of Islamic progress.

Muslim scholars, like those in the West, have formulated conditions for the just use of force. These conditions include just cause, declaration of intention with an invitation to convert, right authority, and conduct of warfare in accordance with Islamic values, which includes fighting with upright intent in the path of God, promoting a just peace, discriminating between the guilty and the innocent, and using minimum force.

The Islamic view of war compares well with the Western just war tradition, but there are differences. Sunnis consider war for religion to be a just cause. Shi'ites and the West do not. All agree that the use of force must be proportionate and that noncombatants should not be directly targeted. Islamic thinkers exhibit this concern in arguing that *jihad* must be fought in accordance with Islamic values, although we must admit that what Muslims mean by noncombatants may not include everyone we in the West would include.

Both the Islamic and Western traditions agree that right authority must be in place. Not just anyone can declare war or *jihad*—he or she must be a legitimate ruler. The classical Islamic tradition treats the guilty and the innocent in war differently than the just war tradition. Guilt and innocence for Islam are decided in part by religious and political factors, and this often appears to Western eyes to be a form of unjust warfare.

Nevertheless, the fact that there are fewer restrictions in the conduct of *jihad* does not mean that there are no rules governing such warfare. The popular belief in the West that crusade or holy war must be distinguished from just war (and hence from wars that are governed by rules of conduct) is simply wrong. The fact that certain wars are divinely sanctioned by no means implies that they are to be fought without restraint. Although there is no single Islamic doctrine of the just war, two things can be posited as holding generally in Islamic warfare: The law restricts wars to combat against injustice, and it requires that combat behavior be consonant with the goal of war, which is justice.

Islamic restrictions on combat behavior were nicely summarized and discussed by the medieval Muslim philosopher Averroes.[3] Enemies were categorized for the purpose of restricting what can be done to different classes of enemy. Women and children, for example, were not to be killed unless they were fighting. Those offered safe conduct were also exempted from attack. Hermits, the blind, the sick, the old, peasants, and serfs were usually exempted from attack as well. Nevertheless, Averroes pointed out how certain traditions argued that all of these may be slain, and this is the crux of the matter.

Averroes identified the controversy in the problem concerning why the enemy is slain in the first place. If the enemy is attacked on account of his capacity to fight (notice the defensive nature of this approach), then the only proper objects of attack are those physically able to do so. On the other hand, if the enemy is attacked on account of unbelief, then we are likely to find no restrictions on who may be slain: All unbelievers are proper objects of attack.

Averroes, it must be pointed out, reflected imperial Sunni thinking on war, and, hence, he was talking about offensive wars of expansion. In such wars, the enemy is given the chance to convert to Islam or, in the case of Peoples of the Book, given the chance either to convert to Islam or pay a poll tax. The major point, however, is that all unbelievers may be proper objects of attack.

MODERN ISLAM AND WAR

While it would be false to say that Islam is a religion of war, it would be true to say that the Islamic tradition has typically been more comfortable with war than has Christianity. Part of the reason is how each tradition views the origin of war and what it means to be human.

In a speech, Ayatollah Taleqani claimed that the role of anger in *jihad* is quite different from any Christian conception.[4] According to Taleqani, God created human beings with the power of anger in order to safeguard the right to live. Anger is a defensive power; it is that which moves you to act in defense of yourself and others. Reason must guide the other faculties, so reason guides anger as a tool to defend rights, territory, dignity, nationality, and so forth. When anger is not utilized in its God-given way, it will become deviant and will result in wars of conquest for material gain and the wanton destruction of other human beings.

Jihad, therefore, is the alternative to mere war and killing. Human beings are going to do one or the other—their innate, God-given anger will drive them either to *jihad* or to mere wars of conquest. *Jihad* is what you do when you use your anger in a God-given way for the purposes of justice, truth, and human liberty. *Jihad* is fighting for the well-being and betterment of human society. Those who die while doing *jihad* are martyrs, but those who die in wars of expansion or gain are not.

According to this view, the problem with Christianity is that it doesn't realize that war is natural and instinctive and thus a human necessity like eating and sex. Christian monasticism, which Taleqani believes is the epitome of Christianity, is not the way of God, because it forbids the human being to do that which it was created to do—to have sex and to make war; and it even curtails eating. To refuse to defend yourself or your loved ones is a failure to strive on the path of God.

MODERN ISLAMIC TERRORISM

Modern Islamic terrorism has as much in common with Marxist teachings as it does with classical Islamic teaching on war. The PLO, for example, has drawn more on the tradition of Arab nationalism and revolutionary "people's war" against oppressors than on the Islamic tradition. In their eyes, Israel and the United States are the unjust imperialists who are out for worldwide imperialism. The PLO does not distinguish the innocent from the guilty in a way comparable with Christian just war doctrine. The PLO's philosophy is basically one of military necessity—doing whatever it takes to win. Thus, any act in war is acceptable as long as it is effective. Anyone who either directly supports the enemy or stands idly by while the oppression continues is a legitimate target.

The combination of Arab nationalism, Marxism, and guerrilla warfare tactics is what marks not only the PLO but Islamic terrorists in general.

Modern Islamic terrorist organizations are unconstrained by classical Islamic prohibitions. They hold to that minority strain identified by Averroes that says that all unbelievers are objects of attack. Modern terrorists, such as Hamas, view themselves as being in the same position as the Muslims who faced Christian crusaders in the Middle Ages. Like Saladin, these irregular warriors attempt, as John Kelsay puts it, to "rid themselves of the rule of non-Muslims and to recover a lost portion of the territory of Islam."[5] The purpose of this sort of *jihad*, therefore, is not expansion but recovery of what was unjustly taken.

Islamic terrorist groups do not limit themselves to Western injustice. This is why *The Neglected Duty*, the "testament" of Islamic Jihad (the Egyptian group that killed Egyptian president Anwar Sadat), argues that any Muslim ruler who does not attempt to live by the traditional law is an apostate not fit to rule; he must be fought. The conduct of this sort of warfare is not set by abstract principles. According to *The Neglected Duty*, the nature of the enemy dictates the kind of fighting that must be employed. Because the established unjust forces greatly outnumber the just forces, there are almost no limits on how the war may be prosecuted. There is no restriction, for example, on killing innocent enemy civilians. This should be avoided whenever possible, but Muslims cannot be held responsible for the consequences of a "legitimate" attack on the enemy.

The tactics of modern terrorists depart from those used by the Muslim heroes on which they are supposedly modeled. This is clearly seen in the use of Saladin as an example of what Hamas and Islamic Jihad are doing. Saladin was famous for his scrupulous behavior toward enemy soldiers and civilians. (In fact, Saladin observed the rules of war much more closely than his famous Christian counterpart, Richard the Lion-hearted. Richard sacked Jerusalem and put Muslim men, women, and children to the sword. When Saladin retook Jerusalem, he spared the Christian population.)

Islamic fundamentalists perceive the West—especially the United States—as evil because America oppresses Muslim people. The United States does this indirectly through its "unjust" support of Israel. American support is seen as unjust in supporting a homeland for Jews that has displaced thousands of Muslim people. The United States also oppresses Muslims through economic policies that favor Westerners at the expense of Third World and Islamic countries.

In the eyes of terrorists, Muslims are in the kind of "supreme emergency" that Walzer wrote about, the kind of emergency that discards moral concerns. The entire Islamic civilization is at stake, and in that situation, as Walzer admits, the innocent become legitimate targets. Because Islamic terrorists truly perceive the West to be such a grave threat to their way of life, they resort to killing innocent people in order to preserve it.

The United States is too powerful for Muslims to fight in a conventional manner; their only option is to strike in such a way that the oppressor will quit oppressing. Random acts of murder are the only effective means available.

Traditional Christian just war doctrine, on the other hand, refuses to defend any notion of doing evil for good to come. Killing innocent people can never be virtuous, can never be sanctifying, and can never bring one closer to God. Classical Islamic laws governing combat behavior also deny that killing the innocent can lead the Muslim to paradise. On this point at least, classical Christian and most classical Islamic accounts of morality in war are in complete agreement.

FIGHTING TERRORISTS

How, then, are we to deal with terrorists? How can we strike back at targets who hide themselves among the innocent?

Once again we must remember that we can never kill the innocent as a means to killing the guilty. The innocent, of course, may be killed as an unintentional by-product of killing the enemy, but in such a case the deaths of the innocent must play no part in meeting the goals of the action.

In striking back at terrorist organizations, we must develop the ability to find where they are hiding. We cannot simply use obliteration bombing tactics as we did in World War II. If we're reasonably sure we know where terrorists are hiding, then we may possibly target those areas, even if their hiding places are populated by innocent civilians. In such a case, it is the terrorists who are targeted and not the civilians. But we still have to count the costs.

How many civilians do we estimate will die as a result of our attack? Does the estimated number outweigh the good sought?

Nowhere are the cardinal virtues more necessary in war than here. The ability to make such decisions requires a great deal of prudence (and mercy). We can only hope and pray that in the current struggle against terrorism, our political leaders, military commanders, and soldiers possess this sort of virtue…and that is hoping and praying for a lot.

Notes

INTRODUCTION

1. C. S. Lewis, *Mere Christianity* (New York: MacMillan Company, 1960), vi.

CHAPTER 1

1. Roland H. Bainton, *Christian Attitudes Toward War and Peace* (New York: Abingdon Press, 1960), 66.
2. John H. Yoder, *Christian Attitudes to War, Peace, and Revolution: A Companion to Bainton* (Elkhart, Ind.: Goshen Biblical Seminary, 1983), 27.
3. For more on the historical consensus and how it relates to recent literature on the subject, see David G. Hunter's essay "A Decade of Research on Early Christians and Military Service," *Religious Studies Review* 18.2 (April 1992): 87-94.
4. In a striking passage in *On Joseph*, Ambrose offers Joseph as a sterling example of the virtuous man who "shows compassion when harmed and forgiveness when attacked," who does not retaliate when force is used against him, and whose conduct "we all have learned after the Gospel yet cannot observe" (1.3). That "yet cannot observe" is what leaps out at the reader. Was Ambrose a proto-Christian Realist, claiming that the rule of the gospel cannot be followed by a politically responsible people? Or was he merely claiming that

our sinful nature hinders us from following the commands of Jesus? The answer is clear from our discussion. The rule of the gospel—the Christian's duty to follow Jesus—still applies. There is no Niebuhrian split between the gospel and the politically responsible citizen, because the rule of the gospel is binding on Christian civilians: Do not use force in self-defense. We can say with some confidence, therefore, that the "yet cannot observe" is a reflection of our inherent sinful nature that makes abstinence from self-defense, a basic instinct in fallen human nature, very hard to achieve.

5. Augustine made this quite clear in his discussion on suicide (*City of God* 1.27) where he argued that one cannot commit suicide even if one's motive is the avoidance of a greater sin.

CHAPTER 2

1. Millard Lind, *Yahweh Is a Warrior: The Theology of Warfare in Ancient Israel* (Scottdale, Pa.: Herald Press, 1980).

2. Lind, *Yahweh Is a Warrior,* 87.

3. T. R. Hobbs, *A Time for War: A Study of Warfare in the Old Testament* (Wilmington, Del.: Michael Glazier, 1989), 17, 211.

4. Hobbs, *A Time for War,* 222.

5. John Goldingay, *Theological Diversity and the Authority of the Old Testament* (Grand Rapids: Eerdmans, 1995), 110.

6. Goldingay, *Theological Diversity and the Authority of the Old Testament,* 109.

7. Goldingay, *Theological Diversity and the Authority of the Old Testament,* 163.

8. Calvin was well aware of the reputation Swiss soldiers had for being good fighters. Swiss mercenaries were a commodity prized by all European armies. But soldiering loses its Christian function and bearing when it becomes a commodity. Calvin realized this and argued vehemently against such practices.

9. C. S. Lewis, "The Necessity of Chivalry," *Present Concerns,* ed. Walter Hooper (San Diego: Harcourt, 1986), 15.

10. Lancelot, of course, did not always behave as the ideal Christian warrior on the field of battle, insofar as he often fought for personal glory as well as for love of God and neighbor. In this regard, the figure of Lancelot represents the tension in popular medieval literature between the secular, chivalric ideal and Christian morality. Nevertheless, the point I wish to make stands: Lancelot is the ideal Christian warrior insofar as he possesses a character equally meek and ready to use force.

11. Lewis, "The Necessity of Chivalry," 15.

CHAPTER 3

1. I owe this point to R. S. Wallace, *Calvin's Doctrine of the Christian Life* (Grand Rapids: Eerdmans, 1959), 122.

2. David Steinmetz, *Calvin in Context* (New York: Oxford, 1995), 116.

3. The analogy between just warfare and surgery breaks down, as do all analogies, if pushed far enough. However, the point of the analogy stands. Acts that are dangerous to bodily life need, if at all possible, to be considered carefully, and this consideration need not imply a moral evil in the acts contemplated.

CHAPTER 4

1. William Tyndale follows Luther on this point in *Obedience of the Christian Man* (1528; New York: Penguin, 2000), 55-9.
2. Peter Geach, *The Virtues* (New York: Cambridge, 1977), 124.
3. Alasdair MacIntyre, "The Wrong Questions to Ask About War," *Hastings Center Report* 10 (1980): 40-1.

CHAPTER 5

1. Stanley Hauerwas, *Dispatches from the Front: Theological Engagements with the Secular* (Durham, N.C.: Duke University Press, 1994), 152.
2. William V. O'Brien, *The Conduct of Just and Limited War* (New York: Praeger, 1981), 47.
3. Robert Osgood and Robert Tucker, *Force, Order, and Justice* (Baltimore: Johns Hopkins, 1967), 290-322.
4. *Nazi Conspiracy and Aggression,* vol. 1 (Washington, D.C.: U.S. Government Printing Office, 1946–8), 119.

5. Eric Lomax, "The Railway Man," reprinted in *The Book of War: 25 Centuries of Great War Writing,* ed. John Keegan (New York: Viking Press, 1999), 450-1.

CHAPTER 6

1. Both "The Justice of the Present War Examined" and "Mr. Truman's Degree" can be found in G. E. M. Anscombe's *Ethics, Religion, and Politics,* vol. 3 (Minneapolis: University of Minnesota Press, 1982).

2. *Target: Germany: The Army Air Force's Official Story of the VIII Bomber Command's First Year over Europe* (New York: *Life Magazine*/Simon & Schuster, 1943).

3. James Childress has gone so far as to say that Walzer's book is "probably the best book on the morality of and in war in the century" (*Moral Responsibility in Conflicts: Essays on Nonviolence, War, and Conscience* [Baton Rouge: Louisiana State University Press, 1982], 64).

4. Michael Walzer, *Just and Unjust Wars: A Moral Argument with Historical Illustrations,* 2d ed. (New York: HarperCollins, 1992).

5. This will always be a debatable point, but for the sake of giving Walzer's consequentialism the benefit of the doubt, I offer no objection here.

6. Karl Barth, *Church Dogmatics* III.4 (Edinburgh: T&T Clark, 1961).

7. In Paul Fussell, *Thank God for the Atom Bomb and Other Essays* (New York: Summit Books, 1988), 13-44.

8. Fussell, *Thank God for the Atom Bomb,* 18.

9. J. Glenn Gray, an army intelligence officer during World War II, reported that "many an American soldier felt shocked and ashamed" when they heard about the use of atomic weapons on Japan. (In *The Warriors: Reflections on Men in Battle* [New York: Harcourt, Brace, & Company, 1959], 199-200).

10. Fussell, *Thank God for the Atom Bomb,* 10.

11. Kenneth Vaux, *Ethics and the Gulf War: Religion, Rhetoric, and Righteousness* (Boulder, Colo.: Westview Press, 1992), 14.

CHAPTER 7

1. Lawrence Freedman, *The Evolution of Nuclear Strategy,* 2d ed. (New York: St. Martin's Press, 1997), 44.

2. Herman Kahn, *On Thermonuclear War* (Princeton, N.J.: Princeton University Press, 1960), 560.

3. Solly Zuckerman, *Nuclear Illusion and Reality* (New York: Viking Press, 1982), 29.

4. Michael Walzer, *Just and Unjust Wars,* 278.

5. John Finnis, Joseph Boyle, and Germain Grisez, *Nuclear Deterrence, Morality, and Realism* (New York: Oxford, 1987), 134-6.

CHAPTER 8

1. Michael Walzer, *Just and Unjust Wars,* 197-206.

2. Jean-Paul Sartre, preface to *The Wretched Earth* by Frantz Fanon, trans. Constance Farrington (New York: Grove Press, 1968), 22.

3. Averroes, *al-Bidayah,* in *Jihad in Medieval and Modern Islam,* trans. Rudolph Peters (Leiden: E. J. Brill, 1977).

4. Ayatollah Mahmud Taleqani, "Jihad and Shahadat," in *Jihad and Shahadat: Struggle and Martyrdom in Islam,* eds. Mehdi Abedi and Gary Legenhausen (Houston: Institute for Research and Islamic Studies, 1986), 47-80.

5 . John Kelsay, *Islam and War: The Gulf War and Beyond* (Louisville, Ky.: Westminster/John Knox, 1993), 97.

Bibliography of Classic Sources

Classic and ancient sources quoted in this book are drawn from the author's own translation as well as from the following:

Ambrose *Discourses on Luke*. In *Patrologiae cursus completus*, series Latina. Paris: Migne, 1845.

————. *Epistle 17, Epistle 29*, and *Epistle 51*. In *Ambrose Letters*, translated by Sister Mary Melchior Beyenka in *Fathers of the Church*, vol. 26. Catholic University of America: Washington, D.C., 1954.

————. *On Duties*. In *Nicene and Post-Nicene Fathers of the Christian Church*, vol. 10, edited by Philip Schaff. New York: Charles Scribner's Sons, 1909.

————. *On Faith*. In *Nicene and Post-Nicene Fathers of the Christian Church*, vol. 10, edited by Philip Schaff. New York: Charles Scribner's Sons, 1909.

————. *On Joseph*. In *Fathers of the Church*, vol. 65, translated by Michael P. McHugh. Catholic University of America: Washington, D.C., 1972.

Aquinas *Exposito et Lectura Super Epistolas Pauli: Ad Romanus*. In *Thomas Aquinatis Operas Omnia*, edited by Roberto Busa. Milan: Editoria Electtronica Editel, 1992.

————. *On Charity*. Translated by Lottie H. Kendzierski. Milwaukee: Marquette University Press, 1960.

————. *Summa Theologica*. Translated by the Fathers of the English Dominican Province. New York: Benziger Brothers, 1948.

Augustine *City of God.* Translated by Henry Bettensen. London: Penguin Books, 1984.

Averroes *al-Bidayah.* In *Jihad in Medieval and Modern Islam,* translated by Rudolph Peter. Leiden: E. J. Brill, 1977.

Basil *Letter 106* and *Letter 188.* In *Nicene and Post-Nicene Fathers of the Christian Church,* vol. 8, edited by Philip Schaff. New York: Charles Scribner's Sons, 1909.

Calvin *Commentaries.* In *The John Calvin Collection (Ages Digital Library Commentary).* Albany, Oreg.: Ages, 1998.

———. *Institutes.* Translated by Ford Lewis Battle. Philadelphia: The Westminster Press, 1960.

———. *A Short Instruction for to Arm All Good Christian People Against the Pestiferous Errors of the Common Sect of Anabaptists (Brieve Instruction).* London, 1549.

Clement of Alexandria *The Teacher.* In *The Writings of Clement of Alexandria,* translated by Rev. William Wilson. Edinburgh: T&T Clark, 1867.

Eusebius *Demonstration of the Gospel.* In *Die griechischen christlichen Schriftsteller.* Leipzig-Berlin, 1897.

Origen *Contra Celsum.* Translated by Henry Chadwick. Cambridge: Cambridge University Press, 1953.

About the Author

Dr. Darrell Cole is assistant professor of religion at Drew University in Madison, New Jersey, and taught previously at the College of William and Mary in Williamsburg, Virginia. A native of Lynchburg, Virginia, and a graduate of Lynchburg College, he holds master's degrees in philosophy from Ohio University, in religion from Yale University, and in theology from Duke University, and he holds a Ph.D. from the University of Virginia.

To learn more about WaterBrook Press and view
our catalog of products, log on to our Web site:
www.waterbrookpress.com

WATER BROOK
P R E S S